T0294927

Workplace Bullying

Workplace Bullying

Finding Your Way to Big-Tent Belonging

Dorothy Suskind, Ph.D.

ROWMAN & LITTLEFIELD
Lanham • Boulder • New York • London

Published by Rowman & Littlefield
An imprint of The Rowman & Littlefield Publishing Group, Inc.
4501 Forbes Boulevard, Suite 200, Lanham, Maryland 20706
www.rowman.com

86-90 Paul Street, London EC2A 4NE

British Library Cataloguing in Publication Information Available

Library of Congress Cataloging-in-Publication Data

978-1-5381-7208-7 (cloth)
978-1-5381-7209-4 (electronic)

♾™ The paper used in this publication meets the minimum requirements of American National Standard for Information Sciences—Permanence of Paper for Printed Library Materials, ANSI/NISO Z39.48-1992.

This book is dedicated to the employees who are quietly inquisitive, raising their hands to voice a new idea, only to be forced to duck and dodge torpedoes launched by the keepers of the status quo. This book is dedicated to the workers who have mastered their craft to such a degree that their productivity and excellence recalibrate what's possible, placing a large red target on their backs. This book is dedicated to the staffers who call out discrepancies and unethical behaviors and then are driven out of their jobs for telling the truth. This book is dedicated to the more than two hundred victims of workplace abuse who boldly told me their stories.

Most important, this book is dedicated to my husband. Through our thirty-one-year love story, starting in high school, growing through college, and expanding over a twenty-seven-year marriage, he shields me from chaotic winds, offering assurance that even amid great injustice, I am beloved and enough. This book is also dedicated to our two sons. Thank you, Mac, for being the first reader of my drafts and offerer of great insight; and thank you, Charlie, for showing me how to embrace my sense of humor and live fearlessly. And last, thank you to my editor, Suzanne Staszak-Silva, who believed in the work and gracefully guided the process.

Contents

Foreword

Dorothy Suskind, like my wife, was dragged into the bullying experience involuntarily, and who similarly has dedicated her life to helping the afflicted. Suskind is a welcome addition to the community of researchers, practitioners, and activists seeking to expose the secretive world of workplace abuse and its deleterious, undeserved impact on the lives of so many good people.

In our early work at the Workplace Bullying Institute, we spoke of bullied targets reclaiming their dignity at work. I like better the author's challenge to targets to reclaim their imagination as part of rediscovering themselves.

The book is a spirited text, showing that the author is not only co-director of the Southside Virginia Writing Project, but that she is a skilled practitioner of the craft. Its vitality moves the reader through dense content with ease. She invites/challenges readers to use writing to clarify their often ambiguous, confusing experiences as a chapter-ending device.

Hail to the power of telling your story, of breaking the shroud of silence and secrecy from which Dragons derive their sustenance. It is a brilliant tactic.

The author's expertise on workplace bullying is multifaceted. What I find most interesting is her willingness to listen tirelessly to tales told by the bullied Creatives. (That's how we started years ago—listening to over 12,000 individuals. Few others do it. It was our research that preceded subsequent empirical work.) Narratives are the richest data imaginable. Suskind credits 200 individuals who taught her a great deal. This book reflects her qualitative research, doubling as nonjudgmental compassionate empathy.

The book is organized into two principal parts. First, bullying, the phenomenon is described—the who, how, and consequences of it. The second part tells how to reverse its personal impact and tells organizations that toxicity need not be the choice by default.

For the author, the bullying phenomenon is a play called Psychological Terrorism (harkening back to an original synonym coined by the movement founder Heinz Leymann) with a cast of characters playing several roles. She, too, admires greatly the innovative, curious Creatives, the targets of bullying, for their myriad of positive, life-affirming attributes. They are the go-to experts. Dragons, bullies, cursed by grandiosity, envy, and little skill, are controllers who rely on a team of sycophants—"shapeshifters"—to do the dirty work of destroying Creatives. Wisely, she contrasts Leaders from Figureheads, the latter being feckless placeholders in hierarchical organization charts.

Another sophisticated way this book veers from the prototypical, but limited, characterization of bullying as dyadic—the target and the bully—is introducing the "stage crew" who manufacture the enabling toxic work environment required for Dragons to operate. At the time of publication, mainstream media mentions of toxic workplaces have exploded. Finally, bullying is not just about individuals. The place, the setting, matters. Chapter 2 provides eight defining features of such toxicity, including debunking the "we are a family" notion, averted gazes, and putting profits above the well-being of humans.

Suskind appropriates Joseph Campbell's Hero's journey into the plotlines of her stage play. The stages of the bullying-as-war experience unfold as a six-act play: target selection, bully jealousy, the contrived justification for abuse, incremental attacks, escalation, and denouement of banishment. Then there is a comprehensive list of 23 "tools" or tactics in a bully's arsenal to wage the nonphysical war against targets. The toolkit includes lies by gaslighting (which was the Merriam-Webster dictionary's word of the year in 2022).

One of the lesser-known tactics is the Dragons' willingness to undermine the purpose/mission of their organization—for example, by deliberately endangering patients in a hospital—in their obsessive zeal to destroy targeted people, and the sadistic exploitation of targets when their health is compromised. I have seen all these tactics and more in my expert witness work in bullying court cases. I consider Suskind listing the many cruel tactics awareness raising for the public. The first set of chapters ends with a detailed dive into the health harm bullying inflicts on its undeserving victims. To us at WBI, the psychological and stress-related physical outcomes are the motivating forces of the anti-workplace bullying movement. The pain and suffering are unconscionable. Suskind skillfully integrates the constructs of stigmatization and degradation by omnipotent Dragons with inflicting pain on Creatives. From her narrative inquiry research for the book, 17 health-destroying themes emerged, including trauma symptoms, somatic complaints, anxiety, depression, shame, and suicidal ideation.

The next set of chapters offer hope for recovery, both for individuals and organizations. Posttraumatic growth allows abused Creatives to become stronger from their horrific experiences. The author shares in chapter 6 how the act of writing was healing for her. Given her specialty, like in no other work I've seen, the reader (assumed to be a bullied Creative) is led through a six-step explicit guide to healing through writing about the bullying experience. The fascinating sixth step is to try one's hand at fiction to step outside reality.

The gifts keep coming in the inspiring chapter 6. Suskind describes a Ceremony of Rebirth designed to mark the end of the influence of the bullying and bullies on your life. The chapter ends with the invitation to selflessly listen to another traumatized person to validate them and make their story sacred. The perfect metaphor for this delightful chapter is a set of nested Russian Matryoshka dolls, always finding more inside, the deeper one digs.

Organizations, driven by Figureheads, loathe creative innovators. But organizations that thrive on creativity do exist. Suskind elucidates features of those positive workplace cultures distilled from her query of the couple hundred Creatives who were not bullied in some workplaces (or in the bullying workplace when supervised by kind, secure bosses). The challenge is to find settings that make the reader feel alive in a world full of possibilities.

Suskind couples many of the lessons gleaned from her Narrative Inquiry research with her affinity for broader sociological and philosophical concepts in a theoretical framework she dubs Closed Circles and Big-Tent Belonging. The latter approach to satisfy the Creative's need for belonging, a fundamental human need, after all, is to be open and inviting to others with varying perspectives. In such a Big Tent, possibilities obtain. In contrast, Dragons, bullies, create close-knit, Closed Circles, of sycophants held together by fear and loathing of "others." The framework credits Creatives with possessing the Dragon's kryptonite—a satisfying and powerful openness toward others. It is the antithesis of hate. The contrast between hoarding insecure Dragons and expansive, generous Creatives is clear. I couldn't agree more. And I further assert that Creatives, the "salt of the earth," are also morally superior. As Suskind writes, they are the ones "holding the heaviness" primarily because of their goodness.

What a world it could be if bold organizations withdrew support from fear-driven cliques who deliberately harm the innocents. The alternative is to nurture big-hearted innovators, the makers of possibilities, the Creatives. This wonderful book allows one to believe courageous organizations are possible, and are not just the stuff of dreams. My fervent wish is that formerly bullied Creatives find such workplaces to feed their souls.

In the concluding chapter, an epilogue that closes the loop begun with a prior discussion of the Hero's Journey, Suskind ends with perhaps her most important list. It's her advice for Creatives—23 practical things bullied targets can do. It's a list worth adopting.

This book has tremendous range. The multiple lists of practical things to do found therein promise to yield positive outcomes for aggrieved people. Thanks to several hundred bullied targets (her Creatives), Suskind speaks with credible authority about the nuanced experiences they and she have lived. They will say that when reading this book it felt like she was in the room with them all the while, the ultimate compliment. And they will take away hope and a sense of personal agency renewed. With that confidence, new life narratives await.

Gary Namie, PhD
Co-founder and Director
Workplace Bullying Institute

Prelude

Welcome.

I am glad you're here.

You may have stumbled onto this book because you are trying to make sense of what happened to you or someone you love, or maybe you are in a leadership position attempting to clean up a work culture that has turned toxic. Perhaps you have spent the past six months Googling "gossip," "gaslighting," and "character assassination" while your mind races with whys and whats:

- Why am I suddenly being left out of meetings and then punished for not being there?
- Why are colleagues I have eaten lunch with for years suddenly icing me out?
- Why is Human Resources retaliating against me for voicing concerns about ethical violations at work instead of investigating the problems?
- Why am I suddenly being put on a PIP (performance improvement plan) when I have been a top employee at my organization for decades?
- What can I do to turn a toxic culture into a productive, innovative, and safe place to work?
- What is happening to my mental and physical health?

As your fingers move across the keys, frantically typing in new search terms, a common theme starts to emerge, and that reckoning provides you with a momentary sense of relief as you discover a name for your experience: "workplace bullying."[1]

Workplace bullying is the degradation of a person's character through gossip, manipulation, sabotage, gaslighting, exclusion, and ostracization with the goal of driving the person out of a job. Jerry Carbo, president of the National Workplace Bullying Coalition, defines it this way: "Workplace bullying is the unwanted, unwelcome abuse of any source of power that has the effect of or intent to intimidate, control or otherwise strip a target of their right to esteem, growth, dignity, voice or other human rights in the workplace."

Naming has great power. To partner a name with an experience validates your lived story. It says that although your plotlines are unique, the basic narrative structure is a familiar construct across countries and continents.

But now that you have paired a term with the trauma, how do you dig into what happened to you, garner clarity about the unfolding, and start to chart a path forward to healing and transformation?

This book invites you to do just that. Right now, your bullying experience likely seems so nonsensical, the preposterous nature of it all leaving your head spinning, your heart hurting, and your mind questioning what might happen next.

But here's the good news—and yes, there are slivers of good news here—workplace bullying follows a predictable cycle, implemented by a known cast of characters, carried out in work environments with shared characteristics. When you look at the research, across case studies, countries, and continents there is a stunning repetitiveness. It is like the tormentors all joined together at the How to Bully People at Work Conference and attended sessions with catchy titles such as "How to Get Your Competition Fired in Thirty Days or Less" and "How to Use Gaslighting as a Tool to Make Your Colleagues Quit."

In the chapters that follow, I will break the code. What once seemed mysterious and incomprehensible will feel familiar and understood. As you read, you will see yourself in the stories shared and find comfort in knowing that this was not your fault, you are not alone, and hope exists on the other side of the mountain.

WHAT IS A CREATIVE, AND WHO ARE THE DRAGONS?

When you read research on workplace bullying, those who suffer attacks are often referred to as victims or targets. Both terms have validity and are useful descriptors. However, on our journey, though I will at times use those terms, I will most often refer to these brave souls as Creatives with a capital C.

I do this for a number of reasons. First, I am a creativity researcher, and part of the study you will read about in this book invites people to tell a story from work in which they were encouraged to think big, take intellectual risks, and engage in innovation. Second, as you will soon discover, though bullies target people for myriad reasons, a salient theme is this: the person is different in how she thinks, looks, speaks, processes, or engages, and this difference enrages the Dragon, for her power relies on predictability and control.

When conceptualizing Creatives, I encourage you to think past the artists and musicians, though these individuals certainly ooze innovation. Instead, conceptualize creativity as the propensity to look and experience situations uniquely, seeing the world anew, thus noticing problems, offering solutions, and practicing empathetic care in a way that is both beautiful and original.

You will also notice that I refer to the bully as the Dragon, a fire-breathing, vindictive character with a mission to control others, an enacted strategy to soothe her suspicion that she is not enough. For when you commit to making others appear small, the mirror temporarily allows you to feel mighty.

A deeper description of both terms will be explored in chapter 1.

WHO THIS BOOK IS FOR

This book is for targets of workplace bullying who have been dismantled by the terror incurred in their hospital, school, university, nonprofit, company, or organization and are trying to make sense of what happened. This book is for bystanders who stood as silent witnesses as a peer was psychologically abused on the job, wanting to help but not knowing what to do. This book is for leaders who watch over a toxic department, blinders tight, unequipped but hopeful to stop the infestation. This book is for families and friends who watch their loved ones lose their passion, inquisitiveness, spark, and ultimately their health to a Dragon who uses gossip, sabotage, gas-lighting, and exclusion to denigrate their character and push them out of a job they loved and excelled at. This book is for you, reader, an invitation from me to understand what workplace bullying is, how it plays out, why it happens, how to stop it, what steps to take to gently heal, and how organizations can craft inclusive cultures that foster creativity and innovation.

As you read, you will notice that though this book is intended for a wide audience, I often talk directly to targets of workplace abuse. This is partially for clarity, allowing me to keep a parallel structure, but also because they are the ones in the spotlight. If you have not been bullied on the job but are trying to understand the experience of those who have, you may find the research more impactful if you attempt to put yourself in the shoes of those who have deeply suffered, to view the stories as a victim, not just an observer.

WHO AM I TO PARTNER WITH YOU ON THIS JOURNEY?

So, who am I to partner with you on this journey?

First, I, too, have experienced the trauma of workplace abuse, and I, like you, had no name to pin on the tornado that tore apart my benevolent worldview and left me with a deep sense of loneliness and despair. I am also an assistant professor at Longwood University in Farmville, Virginia, where in addition to teaching classes in education and women as disruptive change agents, as well as serving as the Director of the Southside Virginia Writing Project, I conduct research on workplace abuse.

As a narrative inquiry researcher, over the past four years I have collected the stories of more than two hundred Creatives, ranging in ages from 18 to 65, across 10 countries, 35 states, and representing 36 industries, all of whom suffered workplace bullying that most often led to job loss and significant health consequences to include high blood pressure, heart trouble, gastrointestinal issues, migraines, anxiety, depression, PTSD, and for some, suicide. It is impossible to read the story of a mother of an adult child who took his life due to workplace abuse and not understand that workplace bullying is not a personality conflict, it is not teasing, it is not a natural part of a competitive work environment. Workplace bullying—and let me be crystal clear here—is a career-altering, life-threatening, debilitating assault on one's humanity.

Due to my own workplace bullying experience and listening to the traumatic stories of others who have suffered abuse on the job, I promised myself, and those who bravely shared their experiences with me, that I would dedicate the remainder of my career to listening to Creatives' stories, providing support for those who have suffered, educating work communities about the cycle of workplace abuse, and helping organizations craft cultures that are both innovative and caring.

To that end, I serve on the executive board and research team of the National Workplace Bullying Coalition and am its acting education director. In addition, I am a contributing member of the International Association of Workplace Bullying and Harassment. I am also a regular contributor to *Psychology Today*, where I predominantly write articles on workplace abuse. My narrative inquiry study you will be introduced to in this book is simply the beginning of a much larger narrative. I intend to continue this study for the duration of my academic career, because people's stories have the power to create positive change. In the next chapter, we will dive deeper into my study and the larger body of research on psychological terrorism at work.

I DIDN'T WANT TO WRITE THIS BOOK

I didn't want to write this book. I had to. As a researcher, my topics arrive at my door and whisper, suggest, and then demand to be told. It is a gift to do the work your soul insists on. But I didn't want to write this book. I said no to myself, to my family, and to my colleagues who entertained my early musings. The work simply hurt too much, breaking my heart each time I engaged.

Then it would happen: an email would appear in my inbox from a grief-stricken mother, on the other side of the world, recounting the suicide of her son who was targeted, taunted, and terrorized by a bully boss while his coworkers stood witness, quiet and complacent, and Human Resources discounted reams of documentation chronicling the terror. Next, over coffee, a friend would recount how after ten years of productive, award-winning work at her company, the new boss was putting her on a performance improvement plan

(PIP), clearly intimidated by the positive spotlight frequently shone on her accomplishments. Then an article would pop up on my feed, detailing the sweeping expenses entailed by workplace cultures that tolerate bullying, manifesting in a lack of productivity and innovation, stagnation, talent loss, and legal fees.

Next, I would overhear the woman in front of me at my local coffee shop sharing how she was leaving her job due to her boss's daily belittlement, sabotage, and siege on her autonomy. As these stories were told, the Creatives' pain was amplified by the surprise of the unfolding. However, as a researcher, I have come to understand that the bullying cycle is not surprising at all but is quite predictable. It is as if all of these abusers had the same playbook. And that is good news, because what is predictable can be called out, rallied against, and stopped. For that reason, I had to write this book.

But—I never wanted to write this book.

WHY I WROTE THIS BOOK

I wrote this book for five reasons: To make the opaque transparent, to build community, to give hope for a better way and a way out, to use art as a tool to heal, and to open the door to innovation.

Make the Opaque Transparent

Most of us have suffered moments of insurmountable loss, cascades of emotions that debilitate our functionality, plummeting us into the grief cycle that Elisabeth Kübler-Ross detailed in her work with terminally ill patients. This research continues to give doctors, caregivers, and patients a shared vocabulary and suppositions for the tumultuous journey ahead. Kubler-Ross's descriptive stages help to set our expectations, making us feel less alone as we fall into the various stages of denial, anger, bargaining, depression, and acceptance.[2]

What if targets of workplace bullying were given similar expectations to prepare them for the fight? What if Creatives knew that they were targeted not for their weakness but for their strength, kindness, innovation, and independence? What if Creatives recognized that the colleagues they once called friends would witness their abuse and stand in silent solidarity with the abuser, possibly joining in the attacks? What a difference it would make if Creatives understood that they would most likely be alone on the battlefield, as Human Resources busied to cover the aggressor's tracks, offering no hope nor support. What if Creatives realized that the Dragon's power is dependent on silence, shame, and compliance—and that plan falls apart when brave people join forces and start to talk? This book is about speaking out.

Build Understanding and Community

Creatives are productive, imaginative, independent thinkers, not interested in playing office politics or joining in on the gossip at the watercooler. They naturally try out different lenses as they work to solve problems, eager to not simply re-create the dusty protocols taped to the conference room wall. Focused forward on "what might be," they don't notice the hand holding the knife. Dumbfounded that last week's cordial colleagues have joined the battle against them, they sit alone at the lunch table, bewildered by their circumstance and sickened by the toxicity. Lacking the vocabulary to understand the phenomenon, they start to shrink, wrongly blaming themselves instead of the workplace culture, players, and circumstances.

This book is an invitation for Creatives to see themselves in the stories of others and join a community that is learning to understand, address, and stop the abuse, opening up new ways to grow and become.

Give Hope for a Better Way and a Way Out

Targets of workplace bullying are often hardworking innovators, their minds overflowing with ideas of how to teach, lead, care, and create inside their organization. When they are targeted by a bully, their first inclination is to give her the benefit of the doubt, work harder, and attempt to rise above the toxicity of the culture that tolerates such behavior. As the bullying intensifies, instead of fighting back or speaking out against the degradation, they double down on their commitment to the organization, dedicating themselves to serving others. When their character is assassinated, their work sabotaged, and they are excluded from company meetings and social events, they look inward, posing the questions: How can I do better? How can I make my boss like and appreciate me? How can I keep this job?

However, though this introspection is admirable, it catches Creatives in a dangerous loop of trying to fix a problem that is likely not within their power to fix, for it is deeply ingrained within a culture that has no intention of changing. Therefore, this book invites Creatives to ask new and transformative questions like: What do I want to do in this world to serve? Where and with whom can I best do that work?

These new questions take Creatives by the hand and lead them toward endless possibilities, seeing their world anew and offering a vision of a kinder, brighter future that may or may not be within their current employment. These questions charge Creatives of workplace abuse to grab onto the best parts of themselves and expand instead of sitting in the corner shrinking from despair.

This book is about hope when things seem so very hopeless.

Use Art as a Tool to Heal

The burnt grass peeks up, weary and longing, as I round the third corner of the Back Bay trail, which runs alongside the Atlantic Ocean, offering a respite for wildlife against the noise and demands of tourists passing by. This trail is my companion and thinking place where I belt out tunes along with the artists on my iPhone, debuting my album of off-pitch songs for the birds. I pass a woman standing by the seaside, capturing her eye's picture in acrylics. The experience invites my five senses to a robust telling that could not be confined to the words of an essay. Diverse telling across mediums evokes a visceral response. Throughout this book, you will experience poetry and creative narratives that share the story of the research garnered from the literature and the more than two hundred Creatives who spoke up.

This is also an invitation for you, the reader, to experiment by telling your story through new tools.

Open the Door to Innovation

The book is a circular story, beginning with innovation that attracts attacks, moving into isolation, and then reclaiming the spirit of originality once again as the Creative either transforms a toxic, stagnant culture, or more commonly, moves to higher ground where she discovers herself again. In this second act, imagination takes center stage and reinvention is upon us. The Creatives you will meet in this book were not targeted because they were underperforming and meek. Quite the opposite: they came under siege because they knocked the status quo off kilter, shook the hierarchy, and attempted to create something that always had the potential to be but was covered tightly by those who benefit from repeating yesterday's mediocrity.

AN EXPLANATION AND DISCLAIMER

You are about to embark on tellings primarily grounded in narrative inquiry, a research method that examines experiences through storytelling. This book is told across mediums and disciplines, honoring the creative processes that the people who shared their stories with me fought fiercely to engage. As you walk through the pages, traditional narratives are disrupted with scripts, poems, diary entries, and streams of consciousness. These genres are the stories and voices represented in the literature and of the women and men who participated in my study, diverse in ages, experience, occupation, income, and geographic location. The format charges you, the reader, to slow down and listen to the stories of our sisters and brothers who showed up in their naked voices to tell the truth.

Stories were selected because they offer an example of universal themes that emerged from my research and the larger literature, insight into the problem of workplace abuse, or a whisper of hope to those struggling to heal. As part of my research protocol, names and identifying information have been changed to maintain anonymity. Some stories have been blended into composites to mask identity and exemplify a theme. Occasionally, direct quotes have been edited for clarity or to remove identifying information that would breach the Creative's privacy. Parts of this book are written in first person, not as a representation of me but as an encapsulation of the voices who have been targeted and terrorized while others watched, blind and frozen in compliance.

It is also important to share that I believe many caring, forward-thinking, and ethically guided individuals work within Human Resources, though at times in this book I present Human Resources in an unfavorable light. This does not reflect my disdain but is instead an outgrowth of a consistent, salient theme throughout my research. Almost without exception, the people who told me their story of workplace abuse had reached out to Human Resources numerous times for help and were met by a closed ear, followed by retaliation.

I think this response reflected less on the character of the people working in HR and was more a symptom of their ability to deal specifically with workplace abuse, which is quite different than addressing issues of employee performance. Therefore, it is imperative that performance and abuse are not conflated.

I believe that due to HR's conflict of interests and reporting structures, it simply is not the best department for navigating workplace bullying, especially when the boss they report to is the one brandishing the weapon. For these reasons, though many Human Resources departments do an excellent job in recruitment, onboarding, payroll, and policies, just to name a few of the many key functions in which they shine, I do not believe addressing, navigating, and fixing psychological terrorism on the job can or should be in their purview.

THE JOURNEY AHEAD

As an avid reader, I appreciate a roadmap for how a book will unfold. Therefore, I will share a short synopsis of our upcoming journey together. This book is organized into an Introduction and nine chapters, beginning with an explanation of the research, moving into the story cycle of workplace abuse, followed by an invitation to reclaim your narrative, proceeding with the characteristics of creative organizations where innovation breathes and excellence rises, and concluding with reflections and helpful resources to continue the journey.

You will notice that at the end of each chapter, I offer you a writing invitation to garner clarity, spur reflection, and initiate healing. As you travel through this book, you may find it helpful to house your writing in a journal or daybook. If you were to visit my home office, you would see countless rows of daybooks on my shelves, waiting for me to scroll through the chronicled decades of my life's unfolding.

Putting your story on the page, pen to paper, and insisting that what you have to say matters holds great power. So, tell your story boldly, even if you decide to tell it only to yourself. Writing is an act of reverence to our humanity, inviting us to take up space in the world, and letting our voices be known. In this sense, writing, in its purest sense, is a form of resistance, a place to insist on your truth, and an act of faith in a better tomorrow. Remember, you own your story. You get to tell your narrative, and tomorrow's plotlines are grounded in light and hope.

Introduction

Here I define workplace bullying and tell you about my research study in which I collected the stories of more than two hundred people across states, countries, and continents who shared their experiences being bullied in the workplace, and conversely reflect on the types of environments in which their creativity thrived. The voices of these brave sisters and brothers are threaded throughout the book's narrative, offering you first-person insight into what it looks like and feels like to be bullied on the job. As you follow their narratives, you will see that you are not alone; though your story is unique, it shares familiar and predictable plotlines across ages, industries, and geographies.

Chapter 1: The Cast of Characters

In chapter 1, you will meet the cast of characters of workplace bullying. First, you will be introduced to the Dragon, or the bully who directs and orchestrates the attacks. Next, you will meet the Shapeshifters who do the Dragon's dirty work, allowing her to keep her claws clean. Then you will be introduced to the Community Builders, whose go-along-to-get-along attitude make them kind colleagues but also susceptible to following the Dragon's lead. Finally, you will meet the two contenders who oversee an organization. Your place of employment may be run by a Figurehead, interested in power and optics, often making him unwilling to engage in critical conversations about workplace abuse. However, if you are lucky, you may be led by a unicorn, also known as the Leader, who exemplifies a deep dedication to the organization's mission and likely rose to influence due to her tenacity to disrupt the status quo and speak truth to power. She is creative, highly ethical, and hence a strong ally for victims of abuse on the job.

Chapter 2: The Setting of the Battlefield

In chapter 2, you will visit a variety of workplaces with toxic cultures. Setting is important, for as stated earlier, bullying, at its core, is not an individual act that happens within a vacuum but a work culture that is promoted and maintained by environments that tolerate and sometimes encourage bad behaviors. Such work cultures tend to enforce strict group norms that stress homogeneous thinking, practice micromanagement, and maintain a steep, impenetrable hierarchy that lacks transparency and discourages collaboration across departments and specialties.

Chapter 3: The Plotlines that Drive the Conflict

Chapter 3 is robust. I begin by recounting Joseph Campbell's hero's journey, connecting the characters and plot to the cycle of workplace abuse.[3] To bring the research to life, I tell the story of June, a participant in my research study, a telling that invites Creatives to see themselves in the plot of another, showing them that what happened, though tragic, was not unique. I then break down the predictable cycle of workplace abuse using the framework of a play in six acts:

1. She Doesn't Belong Here: Target Identification
2. Let's Be Frenemies: Jealousy and Case Building
3. Blame Her: The Precipitating Event
4. Watch Your Back: The Underground Battle Begins
5. Kick It Up a Notch: Mobbing and Escalating Attacks
6. You Are Out of Here: Exit and Cover-Ups

Chapter 4: The Tools of Destruction

Chapter 4 opens the Dragon's toolbox, explaining how she wields her weapons of war. I begin by highlighting her eight primary tools: humiliation and belittlement, gossip, smear campaigns, exclusion, sabotage, gaslighting, ostracization, and retaliation. Next, I share fifteen additional tools she unleashes on the battlefield. Each represents a theme that emerged from my data and is partnered with the voices of Creatives who were the recipients of the attacks.

Chapter 5: This Job Is Making Me Sick

Chapter 5 explores the significant health consequences that victims of workplace bullying experience. I begin by exploring what it means to be stigmatized or have one's sense of belonging to a community shattered. Next, I adopt the lens of a degradation ceremony to explain workplace abuse in which a Creative's humanity is dismantled as a tactic to get her out the door; subsequently, she succumbs to significant physical and emotional suffering as a result of the assault. The chapter concludes with an exploration of the specific physical and emotional health consequences inflicted on those who are terrorized on the job, including but not limited to heart palpitations, high blood pressure, gastrointestinal issues, migraines, depression, anxiety, complex PTSD, and in the worst of times, suicide. As in the previous chapter, Creatives' voices are woven throughout the narrative.

Chapter 6: Reclaiming Your Narrative: Post-Traumatic Growth after Trauma

Chapter 6 is a declaration of hope, offering new possibilities for joy and transformation, proclaiming that all is not lost and our best stories are yet to be written. This chapter provides a roadmap to readers for working through the trauma of workplace bullying, reclaiming their story that was hijacked inside the abuse, and using writing as a tool to move toward post-traumatic growth. Throughout this chapter, readers will hear how victims of workplace bullying took what was meant to harm them and turned it into an opportunity to serve their community and heal themselves.

Chapter 7: Characteristics of Creative Cultures

As stated earlier, bullying is not an individual act carried out in a vacuum but a series of behaviors that transpire in toxic cultures that allow, and sometimes encourage, bullying behaviors. To that end, chapter 7 explores the characteristics of creative cultures and spaces where victims of workplace abuse can reimagine their purpose and expand in new directions. The chapter wraps up by offering detailed steps organizations can take to transform toxic cultures into innovative, productive work spaces.

Chapter 8: Closed Circles and Big-Tent Belonging: A Theory of Workplace Bullying

Chapter 8 takes all of the pieces of the landscape, broken up by the clouds looming above, and pieces them back together as a devastatingly beautiful creation that emerges from the fog. Here the concepts introduced in previous chapters are coupled with the theory that, at its core, workplace bullying is about different interpretations and efforts at belonging with the Dragon creating closed circles to keep out others and the Creative hoisting a flag above a ginormous tent signaling that everyone is welcome here. Between the two camps, Scarcity and Abundance enter the ring to fight for the title that will determine the culture of work.

Chapter 9: Concluding the Hero's Journey

Chapter 9 concludes by zooming in on the last part of the hero's journey, when the main character claims the elixir and brings it back to her community, offering new hope and possibilities. The chapter is told through a series of genres, wrapping up what we learned, offering hope, and sharing helpful resources for moving forward.

In closing, I leave you with a poem capturing the collective voices of the curious creatives as they reflect on what they wish they had known prior to stepping onto an invisible battlefield, completely unaware that the bully war was beginning to brew.

I WISH SOMEONE HAD TOLD ME

I wish that someone had told me my curiosity-covered footprints left behind as I leaped atop my grandma's kitchen table to launch my new ideas into the galaxy would one day be used as evidence in a case against my big thinking. My grandma squealed with delight when I constructed entire cities out of pots and pans, proud of my urban sprawl. I wish I had known that Dragons hate building; their power depends on me playing small. I won't work in a place that makes me shrink.

I wish someone had told me that the woman who recruited me locked secrets in the top drawer of her mahogany desk, planted cameras in the corners to record the proceedings, and dictated seating arrangements to manipulate the narrative. I wish I had known that she carefully crafted a culture that honored uniformity, expected mediocrity, and encouraged gossip as a tool to keep leashes short and taut. Communities that squelch questions have a great deal to hide.

I wish someone had told me that the colleague I hired to offer me support threaded our meetings with rumors and toiled to promote her agenda, driven by self-loathing instead of a commitment to those we served. I wish I had smelled the deceit in the treads of her sandals and recognized the tickets that she was selling to the alternate reality that afforded her power.

I wish someone had told me that when I initiated the construction of big-build ideas, the departure from tradition would make me the target of attacks. I wish I had anticipated that my colleagues who shared my ingenuity would sheepishly retreat when I came under fire, denying support for our co-constructed vision.

I wish someone had told me that the battle against complacency is lonely, that my peers who witnessed the violence would boldly proclaim no recollection of the war. I wish I had understood that Human Resources lacks humanity and withholds resources, primarily to camouflage the boss's incompetence and vengeance. I wish I had known that our communications director was a fiction writer, adept at telling fairy tales.

I wish someone had told me that the emotional warfare and character assassination would not subside when I announced my resignation but, instead, intensify as the institution set off elaborate smokescreens to cloud the toxicity that made me leave. I wish I had anticipated that not one of my colleagues would offer kindness or support, despite my sixteen-hour workdays dedicated to their care. I wish I had figured out that the gaslighting that made me feel alone, inferior, and not up to the job was all part of the manipulation to eliminate me, the one she considered her competition, though I never wanted her job.

I wish that day I packed up my office while security watched, offering no hand with the boxes, the predictability of my predicament as storied through the research. Knowing the plotline would've allowed me to anticipate the scope and depth of her rage. The wheel turns like this: I was targeted for my competence, creativity, independence, and ethics—all of which made me difficult to control. It was spurred by her jealousy that impeded her ability to lead; initiated by unannounced meetings where lies were launched;

intensified by an unwarranted professional growth plan that prohibited growth; escalated by isolation that threatened rebuke to those who offered support; legitimized through character assassination carried out through mobbing; and wrapped up by being pushed out while peers, administrators, and those charged to care cried amnesia for their participation.

I wish someone had told me that the stomachaches, migraines, and deep feelings of despair were not signs of weakness but symptoms of complex PTSD, brought on by months of covert attacks, apparent to all those courageous enough to see. I wish I had recognized that gutting my moral compass was a prerequisite for keeping that job.

I wish someone had told me that discussions and disclosures strip the Dragon of her power. She cannot survive once we talk.

I wish someone had told me that we don't need an invitation to tell our story.

Introduction

BEAUTIFUL RESEARCH AND OUR CRITICAL STORY

You may be tempted to skip this introductory chapter on research; after all, who wants to read dull paragraphs on methodology? I hope you will reconsider. As a Creative, I have come to see research as both naked and beautiful. A cleansing occurs when you let the stories that have gnawed at your insides leak onto the page. I call these essential and provocative tellings critical stories. Once spilled, story lines that initially seemed nonsensical begin to take on a formable shape. That configuration, although unique, shares similarities with others who have plotted a similar path. As researchers, we call these shared experiences a phenomenon, and they include things such as natural disasters, sexual assault, divorce, or in the case of this study, workplace bullying.

As a reader, you may be working under the supposition that the researcher must maintain separateness from her research, observing it from afar, delineating its findings as a cold observer. That's not the case here. This study germinated from my own experiences and then grew up and out from the stories of others. We call this type of journey autoethnography. You may also be concerned that reading research is boring, and certainly at times it is, but that need not be the case, for it is unnecessary to wring the passion out of our world's work and share it grayly on the page, flesh void of color. As a narrative inquiry and autoethnography researcher who studies the phenomenon of workplace bullying, I use art-based research (ABR) to tell the story of the study, meaning that you will find poetry, flash

fiction, stream of consciousness, and other genres threaded throughout the proceeding pages.

   With that brief introduction, let's dive into the details. I will begin
by discussing critical stories and then move into a description of the
four research frameworks: narrative inquiry, phenomenology, autoethnography, and art-based research. I will conclude the introduction by deconstructing the story of the study told across the pages
of this book.

CRITICAL STORIES

We are each called to story.

   Storying is a verb. It is the act of discovering who we are within
the larger plotlines of our community. A critical story is not our
everyday telling of carpools and lunches but the raw recordings of
the moments that shape our existence. Critical stories, sewn into
the seams of our jackets, document our difference and deference.
Our lives, in this sense, are not a collection of isolated events but a
slow-motion montage interwoven through memories. Some flutter
in and out whereas others remain on replay in our mind's recorder.
This fading out, in, and together determines how we process our
lifetimes laden with victories and brokenness.

   My critical story is one of dancing on the periphery of the camp-
fire, not quite belonging. I instinctively made unique connections
across experiences and specialties and shared my eureka artistically,
mesmerized by every day "whys" that frame a childhood. My critical story of "what ifs" was nurtured by Mrs. Paulette, my middle
and high school art teacher, who delighted when I pushed boundaries and painted renditions not at all representative of the world most
people saw. In her classroom, she scrapped the syllabus and simply
cleared the table for me to work, offering instruction and inspiration
but never mandates in how to grow into and past myself.

   My critical story was further supercharged by Jane Hansen, my
doctoral chair at the University of Virginia, who invited me to show
my learning across specialties and mediums, teaching me that when
people "show that know" creatively they both deepen their understandings and broaden their perspectives, lessons I took into elementary through graduate school classrooms where I have taught.
As an adult, I continue to hold tightly to the questionings of a kid.

However, despite a collection of strong women who helped me grow into the boldest version of myself, I, like many of you, also encountered individuals and armies who were jostled by my inquisitiveness, interpreting my questions as direct threats to their self-constructed hierarchy and traditions.

Many of us experience these chapters of emotional abuse, discharges of others' pain, that leave us alone on our front porch as former friends flee for fear of being targeted next. As compassionate beings, we dedicate countless hours attempting resolution—sitting in circles, sharing coffee, or walking around campus. Unfortunately, what I have learned, and research supports, is that colleagues who consistently bully are seldom introspective and rarely remorseful, leaving reconciliation as a distant hope.

Today, I am a full-time assistant professor at Longwood University in Farmville, Virginia. Over the past four years, I have asked more than two hundred people, spanning continents and occupations, to share with me two simple but profoundly complex critical stories: a time they were subjected to workplace bullying and an experience working in a culture that encouraged creativity and intellectual risk taking.

For my study, workplace bullying is defined as an attempt to denigrate a person's character by dismantling her reputation through gossip, manipulation, sabotage, exclusion, ostracization, and gaslighting with the ultimate goal of pushing her out. Another way to conceptualize the abuse: workplace bullying is the charming, manipulative guest who crashes your party, claims she was invited, and leaves your house in disarray after activating each guest's insecurities and establishing a clear hierarchy that places her as the power broker and you as an outsider in your own home.

Creativity, on the other hand, is the whimsical partner who invites you into a new dimension, handing you glasses that allow you to see a new, better reality that brings unexpected people and ideas together for a common goal and purpose. For this study, creativity refers to the ability to uncover hidden connections across disciplines and generate novel solutions to culturally valued problems using diverse tools and mediums.

As a researcher, I listen to people's stories, dissect their plotlines, put my head to the pavement to hear the whispers of emerging themes, and then retell their stories to capture the essence of a phenomenon. Narrative inquiry, phenomenology, autoethnography, and art-based research (ABR) are my chosen frameworks and methodologies. So, what exactly does that mean?

NARRATIVE INQUIRY

According to Connelly and Clandinin, "Humans are storytelling organisms, who individually and collectively lead storied lives. Thus, the study of narrative is the study of the ways humans experience the world."[1] The process is both recursive and reflective, starting in the community listening to the critical stories of Creatives and moving to field notes rewritten in story format, including plots and characters.

Narrative inquiry reflects the multilayered complexity of people's lived lives by inviting research texts that use diverse genres and mediums to tell the story of the findings, including metaphors, poetry, and textual collages.[2] As the poet Okri shares, "We live by stories, we also live in them. One way or another we are living the stories planted in us early or along the way, we are also living the stories we planted—knowingly or unknowingly—in ourselves. We live the stories that either give our lives meaning, or negate it with meaninglessness. If we change the stories we live by, quite possibly we change or lives."[3]

PHENOMENOLOGICAL RESEARCH

Once we understand how we construct the plot of our critical story, infused with our own cultural insights, we are ready to jump on the jet and fly away from our comfort spot in the village to explore a phenomenon, void of our own judgment and through the eyes of those who believe in and were impacted by its existence. After all, our job is not to explain the phenomenon but to provide a rich descriptive story from the perspective of those who experienced it firsthand.[4]

Phenomenological research is spatial, temporal, and relational—situating itself in a specific place, at a moment in time, among others who witnessed the phenomenon.[5] To enter others' critical stories, we ask open-ended questions to invite unbounded space for participants to tell about their experiences. The goal of a phenomenological study is to provide the inside story from those who experienced the phenomenon firsthand. By collecting multiple tellings from diverse people and perspectives, researchers search for "clusters of meaning" of how the specific experience is seen, felt, and internalized by those who walked inside and survived the aftermath or the essence of the phenomenon.[6]

AUTOETHNOGRAPHY

As young researchers, we were told to keep a D I S T A N C E from the work, so as not to inject ourselves into the creases of the stories we are studying. Yet, even when we claim our omission, our personal and cultural experiences still line the strainer our thoughts run through. In other words, we are always there, standing in the center of what we think and learn. In fact, no neutrality exists inside human existence, and claiming our devotions, biases, and blind spots helps to lend transparency to our findings.

As part of that process of "holding up the mirror," my research is infused with autoethnography. Graphy, growing out of the Latin root graphia, which means to write, joins hands with auto, meaning self.[7] As readers engage with an autoethnography text, they are moved by the writer's willingness to be vulnerable, offer her own epiphanies, often from moments of deep struggle, for most autoethnography tells the story of insights and transformations. As Pelias shares, "Today I want to write my way out of this history, and this is why I write my version of performance autoethnography. I want to push back, intervene, be vulnerable, tell another story. I want to contest what happened."[8]

The Poetics of Relational Research

Living

Listening

Telling

Reliving

Repackaging

Retelling

ART-BASED RESEARCH

I am a watcher, a feeler, intuiting the world around me, relying more on what I sense than what I see and hear. So much of my meaning is formed through aesthetics. I use art and writing to capture the rhythms, intonation, and cadence of the world around me; complexities and empathetic understandings not fully attainable through the confines of conversations and linear texts.

More than twenty years ago, during my doctoral studies, I began to engage in art-based research, as if by instinct, though I had not yet connected the term to my process. ABR offers a different way of thinking and being, living on a larger landscape, inviting a storying approach as it turns over rocks alongside the path in search of meaning. Within ABR, there is an agreement of the fluidity of perspectives based on the experiences of the participants and teller.

In ABR, the critical story of the work is told across genres, each one selected because its qualities fit the emotions, intentions, and truth of what was discovered. Barone and Eisner describe it this way: "Arts based research is not a literal description of a state of affairs; it is an evocative and emotionally drenched expression that makes it possible to know how others feel. In the pursuit of such an aim, the metaphor will be appealed to, analogies will be drawn, cadence and tempo of the language will be controlled, innuendo will be employed, simile will be used to illustrate meaning, and other such devices will be used to create the expressive form we mentioned earlier."[9]

THE STUDY

For the study shared throughout these pages, participants initially shared their stories anonymously through writing and then had the option to leave their contact email for a follow-up interview.

During the first year of my research, I sent the survey to colleagues for distribution and posted it on a variety of private Facebook groups for victims of workplace abuse, with an initial goal of collecting forty narratives. As the year progressed, the study took on a life of its own, prompting me to create a website on workplace bullying called Bully-Wise, which details the study, shares a link for participation, and includes a variety of articles I have written on workplace abuse in addition to other helpful resources.

During the past four years, more than two hundred people have anonymously shared their stories. The Creatives range in ages from 18 to 65 and live in diverse geographic locations stretching across 35 states and 10 countries, representing in total more than 36 different industries.

Today, most contributions come from people visiting my website after participating in a conference or webinar in which I spoke or after reading one of my articles in *Psychology Today*, where I am a regular contributor.[10]

The study setup is fairly simple. Though people's identity is kept anonymous, the first part of the survey asks participants to share basic demographic information including their age, gender, state, country, and occupation. Victims shared their ages by checking one of the following age brackets: 18–25, 26–35, 36–45, 46–55, 56–65, and over 65. Surprisingly, the largest number of participants fell in the 46–55 range (35 percent) with the next largest representative group being 36–45-year-olds (28 percent). In addition, the majority of victims self-identified as women, which is in keeping with the research that men bully women and men in equal measure, yet women are far more likely to bully other women, making women, in general, the most frequent targets of attacks.[11]

Victims also self-identified their occupation, and in total, more than thirty-six different jobs were represented. My findings are in keeping with other studies, in that the largest percentage of victims worked in health care, with most being nurses, closely followed by those working in K–12 schools and higher education.[12] Government workers took third place. The remaining employment sectors were diverse and widespread, including but not limited to marketing, fish hatcheries, aviation, hospitality, finance, advertising, railroads, fitness, and engineering.

For the study, I asked participants three simple but deeply important questions:

1. Have you ever been a target of workplace bullying? If so, please share your experience below.
2. Tell the story of an environment or culture you have participated in that encouraged creativity and intellectual risk taking.

3. If there is any additional information you would like to share, please feel free to share it below.

So, what types of stories did Creatives share about their bullying experiences and those spaces in which they were encouraged to take intellectual risks and innovate? Below are two examples.

I came up with new ways to research and identify which train cars were moving in a train based on comparing the lists of car numbers generated by the train scanner locations. I was praised for my commitment to work and my dedication for years, until a certain person started spreading rumors and innuendo about me, both in our department as well as others. It literally went from one day they were thanking me for my help to all of a sudden, overnight—people quit talking to me, ignored I was even there, and just glared at me when I said hello. She recruited others to be on her side, when all I had done was help correct some errors she had made, since she had created some documents that showed a train as nonhazardous, when in fact it was hazardous, containing military equipment. She took it personally and launched a smear campaign about me for months. It was unrelenting until I finally had a panic attack at work and was fired after 29 years. My career was ruined. —*Railroad Clerk*

Yes. I have an excellent work record. No bad appraisals or warnings. My new boss disliked me because I believe he had an issue with my gender. He changed my working hours (the ones I had worked for 15 years). He gave me a week's notice of the change even though he knew I had family commitments. He did not contact HR regarding the changes saying, "I am your manager I can do what I want." When I objected the bullying escalated. All my work was withdrawn. I was isolated from the team and made to sit in a room with no windows on my own for 8 hours a day. All my emails were monitored as were my phone calls. He told people I was useless at my job. He belittled me and insisted that I had mental health issues. To be honest my job allowed creativity until the new manager started. Alas I am not the only victim from this department. All of us have had breakdowns from the stress. HR has refused to hear my grievance and has fully supported the bullying management. —*Health-Care Worker*

In contrast, here are some stories of innovation that Creatives shared.

I used to work as a correctional officer. I oftentimes had to be creative in the approach I took with the inmates. Every night, we had "Porters."

Porters are inmates who are tasked with cleaning the housing units. I had the nighttime cleaning crew. My group cleaned from 10 p.m. to about 5 a.m.. It was difficult sometimes to get the Porters to be willing to clean and clean well. In addition, I had a Sergeant that would white glove the unit, so I had to stay one step ahead of him. It may not seem all that creative to the average person, but by allowing my Porters to have extra breaks and sometimes let them off "work" early, it helped me keep my Porters motivated to do the deep cleaning my Sergeant liked to see. Sometimes I'd even make sure my Porters were the first inmates to use the showers in the morning since they were the ones who cleaned them . . . the unit had 136 inmates to five showers, and the Porters wanted a shower before they went to bed. —*Correctional Officer*

In my current position, my role is to be there for the students and act in their best interest. I do some crazy stuff in my classroom, such as sitting on the floor with high school students and pretending to be in preschool with silly songs. I am always supported and encouraged to do whatever it takes to help the students learn. —*Teacher*

As stated earlier, after sharing their stories in writing, the Creatives had the option to be interviewed. Though I took extensive notes during our conversations, I did not record the Creatives' names, employers, or other identifying information. To date, I have conducted more than fifty interviews, each lasting on average two hours and some going well over three. Interviews were conducted in person, via phone, or over Zoom.

Because this study is a lifetime calling, I continue to interview one or two victims of workplace bullying each week. I consider it a great honor to hold space for people's narratives. As a narrative inquiry researcher, I simply listen to people's stories, rarely asking questions, so most Creatives recount that they found it quite healing to have a person witness their pain and validate their experience.

The two hundred stories that victims of workplace abuse shared generated more than seven hundred pages of narratives. As a narrative inquiry researcher, I read through the narrative transcriptions in their entirety multiple times, coding pertinent information and searching for emerging themes within stories and across stories. This idea of "emerging" is important, because as a qualitative researcher, I do not enter the work with a set hypothesis or preconceived notion; instead, I trust the stories to reveal their meaning on their own terms. This disposition opens me fully to discovery and surprise. Following the initial coding, similar codes or categories are collapsed into themes. The themes are then used to generate some universal story lines or plotlines that appear within and across narratives. This exercise is reiterative and recursive, a circular process that is ongoing in search of saturation or steady and constantly recurring patterns across narratives.

In summary, each of us has a critical story to tell that overlaps the critical stories of others, creating a community of narratives. As it relates to workplace bullying, understanding community stories provides insights into workplace culture norms. This is important, because bullying, at its core, is not an individual problem spurred by one person but an outgrowth of a workplace environment that either allows or encourages such behaviors as gossip, humiliation, belittling, gaslighting, and exclusion. For this reason, when organizations make the bold move to get rid of a Dragon, yet fail to look inward at the workplace culture norms that support such behaviors, a new Dragon almost always emerges.

Only by changing work cultures can we eliminate workplace abuse. That transformation takes bravery, knowledge, truth telling, and introspection. This work gets done through outward examination, discovery, introspection, and beautiful and vulnerable research, where we create space for people to share the stories that broke their hearts alongside narratives woven with hope and possibilities.

I close this chapter with a poem followed by your first invitation to use writing as a tool for understanding, hope, and healing.

IT TAKES A VILLAGE

This is how you do it
You watch
Carefully
Notice how she walks
Talks
Moves amid the crowd, noting pauses in her confidence
Identify her trigger points and prepared to punch
Smile
Ingratiate yourself
First in small ways that sit on the border of what is expected
Start with daily check-ins to inquire about last night's Little League
Make her feel seen and valued - willing to unlock her defenses, for a
    stolen moment, allowing you access to her tribulations

She shares her struggles with food
You smirk, sock that away in the arsenal
Ammunition
Still churning the cement, you twist the hook to strengthen her devotions
Perhaps a gift card you leave on your desk, the one you screeched at your
   secretary to pick up on her off-hours
Underlings hold no value after all
Over private lunches at your expense, offer up your own testimonials, just
   deep enough to show the tips of your humanity, an elaborate facade
   constructed by observing those who actually feel
As you sip organic tea, tear up recounting your adult daughter's struggles
   with infertility
Embellish with details, pulled from a hat, for your daughter ceased all
   contact with you eight years ago, refusing to drink the poison you
   spilled over her childhood
With the foundation of false care built, start to create cracks
After hours, unannounced meetings work well
Come from a place of care and concern
"Because I care about you and consider myself your mentor, I wanted to
   let you know that at last night's cocktail party people were expressing
   concern over your current project. They don't think you have the skill to
   carry it to the finish line"
It is important that you take what she does best and make her doubt her
   own competencies
Gaslight
Gaslight
Gaslight
She is creative, tell her people think her ideas are dull
She is bold, tell her people think she lacks leadership
She is innovative, tell her people think she is not in touch with the diverse
   culture
When she inquires who these people are - claim sympathetically that you -
   "Are not at liberty to tell, but are certainly still her biggest fan"
Invisible armies wreak havoc on self-perception
Pretend to be her cheerleader not the puppetmaster working to rewrite her
   character out of the script
Over time, she will begin to doubt your motives
Sprinkle her with confidence, restore her value, make her feel guilty for
   doubting your intent
Take advantage of her benevolent assumptions
Now reschedule your typical lunchtime so you have the opportunity to
   break bread with her peers
Drop innuendos in regards to her high levels of stress and fading mental
   capacities

Fein worry
Find yourself in the elevator with her superiors
Sell your pitch
Take ownership for her success projects
Drop airs of concern
Disinvite her from meetings
Punish her for not being there
Alert Human Resources that she has become unreliable
A disappointment
Intensify the underground rhetoric
Battered and demoralized, she will uncover your darkness
It is too late
You have claimed her village
You told her friends she was unraveling
You told her boss her ideas were yours
You told her that everyone at the company hates her (except for you of
    course)
And the damage you inflict elevates her blood pressure, increases her
    migraines, and causes her stomach to entwine into knots
When she takes a sick day, intensify your siege
Demand Human Resources place her on a Performance Improvement Plan
They will balk
For she is a seasoned superstar
Persist
Push
Lie
When she returns
Show no mercy
Remove the mask
Demolish her
Explain to her peers that she has entered "a process"
When they inquire what that means, threaten their livelihood
Insist they cease contact
Demand her isolation
Pile on the work
Make it impossible for her to hit her improvement goals
Kick her
Hard
While she is down
She will plead for Human Resource's help
But will find they are neither human nor resourceful
Enraged - she will seek out your boss
But her tears will only confirm your story that she has become undone
She will turn to her colleagues

For surely her friends will have her back
Yet she will be unfriended, blocked, and left at the table to eat alone
Deemed an untouchable
Even the minister will hear God demand to withhold comfort and support
Deeply spiritual, the depth of the corruption, the length of the lies, the
   bitter taste of mean-spiritedness will shatter her
Into a million pieces
And everyone will simply watch
Afterall . . .
Such destruction takes complacency, shame, and secrecy
It takes a village.

INVITATION #1

Each chapter concludes with an invitation to engage in the chapter's content through written reflection. In this introduction, I shared my critical story initiated as a young child scared to speak out and the transformation that occurred when my art teacher, Mrs. Paulette, opened space for me to tell who I was off the page of tradition, praising my propensity to take intellectual risks. What critical story or seminal event that shaped your later being and understanding of the world do you hold deep in your heart?

Remember, you may find it helpful to keep your reflections in a notebook, for in my experience, magic often transpires on the page when pen meets paper that is not as eager to show up on the keyboard. Feel free to list, draw, and just let your consciousness stream with no judgment or fear of rebuke. Keeping your reflections and wondering together in one notebook will provide you with a chronicle of your growth and transformation.

Chapter 1

The Cast of Characters

THE MASK YOU SLEEP IN

Who are you when you sleep?
In those moments before you awake and clothe yourself in work's
   costumes
Are your feet tiny in those mega heels?
Attempting to appear taller than your doctor's measurement
It is not necessary to stand atop me in order to see
I have no interest in your line of vision
The room is large
Providing infinite space for us all to breathe

In this book, we will think of workplace bullying as a play with characters, settings, and plots. The title of this production is *Psychological Terrorism*, starring six key players who hold pivotal roles in the bullying cycle.

As a narrative inquiry researcher, early in my career I became captivated by the work of Joseph Campbell, a writer and scholar of comparative mythology, in particular his notion of the monomyth explored in his seminal book, *The Hero with a Thousand Faces*.[1]

Within those pages, Campbell details archetypes that include the *hero*, the protagonist who drives the plot; the *shadow*, the antagonist who blocks the hero's positive momentum; the *herald*, who signals the challenges that lay ahead; the *mentor*, who offers wisdom and the necessary resources to overcome obstacles; the *threshold guardian*, who attempts to avert the hero's entrance or progression; the *ally*, who offers the hero assistance in reaching her goal; the *shapeshifter*, who is a master of deception; and last, the *trickster*, who causes ongoing disruption and at times serves as a catalyst for change.

Over the past four years, as I reflected on my own bullying story and immersed myself in the narratives of others who have suffered abuse on the job, coding and recoding more than seven hundred pages of data, my own set of characters started to introduce themselves on the page, each one playing a predictable role, trying out honed tactics, and spinning familiar plotlines. It was quite extraordinary; these characters first revealed themselves as a whisper, and before long, I could see them boldly claiming their spotlight in the story.

Though in my own world, when I am "doing life," I resist the urge to label people, as a researcher charged with making sense of shared phenomena—in this case, workplace bullying—labeling helps to give shape to the shapeless, inviting people to see the similarities in stories across countries and continents.

Then, when I began to share my characters with fellow researchers and victims of workplace trauma, cries of, "Yes, these folks are in my story, too," came out of people's mouths, and that recognition alone helped to diminish Creatives' prevailing sense of hopelessness, because they no longer felt alone on a distant island but, instead, recognized themselves as reluctant participants in an ancient and repeated play.

Further, this typecasting enables victims to identify who they are dealing with, and this familiarity helps them anticipate their tormentors' next moves. As we will see in future chapters, these characters are not particularly original in their actions but, instead, duplicate the same plots continually simply switching their victims.

So, let's meet the characters starring in *Psychological Terrorism*. First, you will meet the Creative, who I suspect is you, uninterested in office politics and resolute in her desire to create a just world. Second, you will spy the Dragon, who directs the tragedy and writes the rules of engagement. Third, you will encounter the Shapeshifters, desperate in their need for power and belonging but lacking in the Dragon's iron will and fortitude, taking on the role of chameleon as they do the Dragon's bidding, allowing her to keep her claws clean. Fourth, you will recognize the Community Builders, beloved by all but willowy, bending to the prevailing winds of power, making them highly susceptible to joining the wrong team. Last, you will meet the official directors of the schools, universities, hospitals, companies, and nonprofits wearing one of two name tags, either Figurehead or Leader. The Figurehead sits on his throne guarding the status quo; the Leader goes to work, placing herself on the firing range, committed to innovation and excellence even if it comes at a cost to her.

With that brief introduction, it is time to go behind the curtain, remove the masks, and get to know the players. Intermixed with their descriptions, you will hear firsthand from the victims of workplace abuse, aka the Creatives, as they describe their interactions and perceptions of the seasoned cast. Because they are the main players, the Creatives and the Dragon will get the most stage time.

THE CREATIVE

> The Creative walks up to the wall, undeterred, draws a circle, cuts a window, and peers out to the fields of untapped potential, which she names Possibility.

Creatives buckle their boots each morning, readying for the journey, independent in their thinking but appreciative of diverse collaboration. Constantly seeking new information, they are amazed by the world around them, eager to outgrow themselves on the path to new discoveries. Appreciative of tradition but not shackled to the past, they exist in a continual loop of reevaluation, not content to spend their careers cleaning up messes but, instead, eager to uncover the source of the spill. Their propensity to rattle the status quo and disregard hierarchies frustrates the Dragon, whose power depends on keeping the gates closed, the conversations regulated, the paths narrow, and the secrets locked safely in her mahogany desk.

Now let's dive into the details of eleven characteristics essential to the makeup of the Creative's spirit, each rising up from the data.

Change Agent

The Creative is committed to evolution, both in himself and his organization, charging him to spend hours untangling the knotty problems that have become institutionalized in his school, university, hospital, government agency, nonprofit, or corporation. Perhaps he is attempting to tackle his students' unprecedented levels of anxiety, not by organizing assemblies on stress management but by diving deep into the curriculum and school culture that is germinating and then nourishing the stress.

The Creative has an innate sense of social justice that makes him willing to give voice to the voiceless and call out inequities that are causing others to play small. However, when he starts to turn over and move the rocks, attempting to widen and flatten the path, consequences are certain to come from those whose power depends on maintaining the steep, foreboding slope.

I have been brought into a number of transformative roles. I was hired to clean up the messes. I always brought positive results and made friends quickly. But then, almost always, I would come under attack by those in power who didn't like the changes. Then they would turn the rest of the department against me. Suddenly, I was the bad guy. Immediately I was the target in each case, even though I always brought positive business results and made friends quickly. Attackers have been men and women. —*Manager*

My desire and ambition accelerated when I attended a Fortune 500 leadership program as an undergraduate, which promoted the motto, "Leaders have a healthy disregard for the impossible." I have grown as an out-of-the-box, persistent problem-solver my entire career. With all humility, my record as a change agent is extremely impressive. I have practiced an extraordinarily high level of creativity, innovation, and moral courage in every endeavor I have pursued. I have been celebrated for my efforts more times than not. Unfortunately, I have been the exact opposite of the conservative, dull-minded, good ole boy networks I often encounter. I have now been a whistle blower multiple times in my career. My efforts to solve complex problems with innovation and creativity have always made me a target; however, I have not suffered irreconcilable repercussions till now. This current saga is the first time I have experienced this level of vitriol. It is truly off the charts. —*Military*

Curious

A Creative's first words are "why" and "what if," looking at the world as if it is a puzzle missing a piece and content to search for its return. She is driven not by promotions and accolades but an innate curiosity that leaves her constantly questioning whether there is a more compassionate, proactive way to serve her students, patients, and clients. This propensity, however, awakens the Dragon.

> They had never been very happy with the fact that I would make suggestions for improvements about process or how we could improve the student experience with e-learning courses. They finally really turned on me when I asked my manager for a role where I could use my expertise (which they refuse to acknowledge) effectively to help the organization's customers. —*Instructional Designer*

Innovative

The Creative's innate curiosity, as just shared, spurs her to take intellectual risks in her quest to solve institutionalized problems using resources, research, and collaborations in unexpected ways. Her proclivity to innovate brings her early accolades and attention, which enrages the Dragon, committed to keeping the spotlight on his own career. In response, it is not unusual for the Dragon to take credit for the Creative's work as he busily attempts to push her out the door.

> I value innovators and companies that believe in moonshots and out-of-the-box thinking. Yet, when I gave my work to my manager, she presented it as her own. —*Health-Care Worker*

Uninterested in Office Politics

The Creative is happy to join anyone in the cafeteria for lunch, eager to hear others' stories. He arrives on the job ready to make something new, content to work alone or collaborate across departments and up and down the corporate ladder. Titles hold little interest for him. He is invigorated by solving work conundrums that have eluded others while working to grow his own craft and expertise. The Creative is a good friend to all and makes a concerted effort to thwart office gossip.

Naturally empathetic, he quickly identifies the social climbers and keeps his distance, instead opting for authenticity, mutual interests, and diverse points of view as foundations for friendship. However, his reluctance to subscribe to the office gossip makes him the last one to know he is the new headline titled Attack.

When I experienced workplace mobbing, I realized I had not been advised on how to navigate the very serious politics that exist in academia. I made some missteps, and as a result, was targeted by some very powerful and influential people. As a professor, it spanned across universities and even countries. I had to leave my job to escape the abuse. —*Professor*

Productive

The Creative arrives early, stays late, and accomplishes more before lunch than some stretch over the work week. She believes that if a job is worth doing, it is worth doing well and in a timely manner. Her propensity to produce at harrowing speeds recalibrates the status quo of what's possible, and this revelation enrages colleagues and supervisors who have become accustomed to late arrivals, feet-up lunches, and a lack of accountability.

> The boss hired people he had a history with. This created a large group of extremely unaccountable, yet loyal, protected staff members. It also created a very unimaginative, intellectually lazy, and corrupt culture. I worked hard to force merit-based hires, hold people accountable, and maximize our ability to achieve excellence. In addition to the tactics described in your research, I have now been the target of over 30 adverse personnel actions during this timeframe. —*Military*

Cross-Collaboration

Creativity and innovation germinate in unexpected corners where people with diverse expertise and experience bring their stories to the table, and inside these multiple tellings, imaginative solutions start to transpire. However, the Dragon's power is dependent on controlled conversations and short leashes, so he is enraged when the Creative has lunch with people who aren't on the approved communication list, for he works overtime to squelch such encounters, or at the very least take credit for their ideas.

> My supervisor got angry that I collaborated with people outside our team. She said I "overstepped," which I hadn't, and then she took the report we created and presented it as her own. —*Finance Manager*

> My headmistress asked me to stop eating lunch with the children in my school. I explained that I wanted to get to know them better and

understand their experiences. She said they were telling me too many things that got me worried. She didn't like the problems they were sharing. She wanted everyone to pretend things were fine. Since I was curious, she saw me as an extreme threat. She tried to isolate me and make sure I didn't talk to anyone who would share the truth. She believed her power was in creating a mirage of excellence. To do this, she made sure nobody talked to each other. Eventually it caught up to her and she was fired. She deserved it. —*School Principal*

Top Performer

The Creative is often hired because of his exceptional work history documented on a résumé that is both long and broad. And though companies are often eager to secure such talent, when this top performer reports for duty, he does what top performers do: he performs. Such performance, however, stirs unrest in colleagues who are content with moving slowly through the halls as they give each other self-congratulatory smiles for reinventing the wheel.

> I had a stellar career with a positive reputation for over a decade. Then, out of the blue, there was an "anonymous" complaint against me and my university suspended me without pay indefinitely pending their "investigation." —*Basketball Coach*

Expert in Their Field

The Creative's curiosity spurs her to tick away the hours reading, researching, and garnering an exceptional level of field expertise, as evident by her multiple degrees, countless publications, and walls lined with accolades. Her deep dive knowledge makes her the go-to person for guidance, collaboration, and advice. Such attention touches the insecurities of the Dragon, who commits to sullying the Creative's well-earned, pristine reputation.

> Competent women are seen as threats. —*Diplomatic Aid Worker*

> My resume and evaluations place me in the top five percent of my peers. It is dispicable [*sic*] how I have been treated. I have been punished for being too good at what I do. —*Military*

Different in Some Way

Creatives have a shine that makes them unusual, a gift that frees their souls from the confines of social expectations. They may be neurodivergent, noticing the intricacies of problems and people in complex ways unavailable to most; or they may dress differently, seeing no need to conform to fashion trends; or perhaps they are part of a minoritized population and won't be cajoled into inhabiting the costumes or customs of the majority. However, they really sparkle when you are with them, exuding a deep and unique authenticity. This difference, however, threatens the Dragon's need for conformity in thoughts, words, and deeds, so she sets out to bring these Creatives into compliance through public humiliation and degradation. Unfortunately, the Dragon will soon learn that Creatives' deep sense of self and independent spirit is not easily intimidated or swayed.

> They started to do things like make fun of my clothes and hair, teasing me for wearing the same clothes every week. I'm a nerdy tech girl and not interested in clothes and brands or keeping up with the latest trends. So I pulled away more, just put my head down and worked and said as little to them as possible. —*Government Foreign Service*

> If you're creative, go above and beyond in your job, are professional, diligent, follow ethics and are female or any other minority you're a prime target. —*Health-Care Worker*

> I was fired and sabotaged by the tenant manager because the tenants preferred me over her and she didn't like it at all. I worked for a Black-owned business and she is white. She submitted falsified complaints from the residents that were all written in her handwriting. I knew because most of them were too old to write regularly and part of my job was to help them with filling out forms, reading mail, etc. —*Writer*

> I now realize the times I've been capable of intellectual curiosity and high levels of creativity all involved environments where my supervision presumed competence and good intentions. They gave me time and space to explore and refine my ("highly unusual," i.e., neurodivergent) processes, and encourage my efforts as opposed to belittling me or the process itself. They never prematurely judged on incomplete results. And, I wasn't getting penalized by being denied access to much-needed opportunities and facilities necessary to do my job. —*Medical Doctor*

Well Liked

When you meet the Creative, you just feel good. He has an innate kindness and a dedication to service that is not tied to recognition, ladder climbing, or monetary gain. Over time, due to the Creative's approachability and accepting demeanor, he becomes a favorite at work. This natural attraction, however, gives him unintended social capital that awakens the Dragon's jealousy, pushing her to degrade the Creative's character in an attempt to convince others that he is, indeed, an untouchable.

> I was aware of the other individuals because our department is very small, and I have always had good relationships with the more senior members. I had at some point also fallen into the mentor role for all of our students and interns/postdocs, in hindsight, obviously because my supervisor (the department head) was not treating them well. Everyone had always seen me as an extremely intelligent, efficient, and conscientious individual and some of my "years of experience" were even waived in my case because of my clinical skills. I had (and still have) an excellent relationship with my old supervisor who is now retired. —*Clinical Psychologist*

> One of the research staff appeared to become defensive due to my good rapport within the team and proceeded to deny all code submissions while projecting questions about my code into the team, and without any substantial evidence. —*Software Engineer*

Highly Ethical Whistle-Blowers

The Creative, at her core, possesses a deep commitment to ethical decision making and compassionately caring for those she is charged to serve, whether they be students, patients, or clients. When injustices are uncovered, the Creative speaks truth to power and blows the whistle on unethical and illegal activity, fully knowing that by speaking out she will be subjected to unwarranted attacks on her career and personhood. For the Creative, telling the truth is an obligation, not a choice.

> Being a registered psychotherapist & Christian, I have to do what's right. —*Psychologist*

I reported a wide range of documented ethics and legal violations occurring at the national level in the association. —*Public Relations Manager*

I became a whistleblower due to malpractice & fraud taking place, which then meant the bullying was instigated by management, HR & even the Principal, who failed to address not only the disclosures made but the staff responsible for departmental bullying, eventually turning the bullying on me, obviously to manage me out of the business. —*College Lecturer*

I've been bullied by two different groups at work from my Chair and the President of my union, and then by a clique in my department who engaged in illegal hiring. —*Professor*

I reported academic misconduct and was told to keep my mouth shut or lose my job. —*Teacher*

In summary, Creatives are change agents who are naturally curious and innovative. They are well-liked and uninterested in office politics, instead committing themselves to being productive cross-collaborators who are top performers and experts in their field. Often, their exceptionalities make them different, standing out above the typical. With a deep commitment to service, when Creatives see something unethical unfolding, they speak truth to power—if necessary, blowing the whistle on bad behavior.

THE DRAGON

The Dragon seethes and then shudders, placing her claw on the linoleum floor, feeling for vibration. She wants to be the first to know who is shaking the hierarchy and breaking the rulebook. Upon identification, she snorts fire, a declaration for the Shapeshifters to load the cannons and prepare for war.

The Dragon writes the unofficial rulebook, posts it on the walls for easy review, and then employs intimidation to assure that the Shapeshifters and Community Builders carry out her mission with military precision. The Dragon's wings and scales are often concealed by designer clothes and a charismatic personality, for she is dedicated to keeping her claws clean as she directs others to sling the mud. Organizations rarely have more than one Dragon, for they will fight each other to the death to secure their seat at the head of the table. If by some good fortune a Dragon leaves the institution, another is sure to command her position, for bullying, at its core, is a cultural construct that tolerates and encourages Dragon behavior.

Low Productivity and Status Quo Thinking

The Dragon, in general, is not innovative; her attention is focused on keeping others in their lane and squelching creative ideas. Because power is the prize, she keeps the reins tight and her playlist set on repeat, for keeping the status quo helps to eliminate surprise and ensures that everyone remains in his assigned seat.

> The art department was reluctant to change or engage in any intellectual risk taking. Their culture was to remain as it had been for years. —*Art Teacher*

> The teacher who holds my same position at another school in my district seems to be threatened by anyone who does not agree with her ideas. We are supposed to collaborate across the school district, and although I reach out to her and a 3rd colleague, they do not include me in their meetings. —*Teacher*

> I quickly saw that the dysfunction my friend described was rampant in this clinic. There was a core of nurses who were close to the management that had much freedom and little responsibility. They never answered their pagers, and I discovered this is because they had gone home very early and were still on the clock. One RN had no title or job description but did not have to do patient care. She was going to school full time and so was getting paid and not at work. The physicians were miserable and without needed supplies. Management knew but only rolled their eyes at repeated requests for personnel supplies. —*Nurse*

Low Skill Level

The Dragon is often hired for his charismatic personality, not his expertise, and then is kept on for his propensity for pulling the puppet strings. He tends to offload work for two primary reasons: first, he is lazy; and second, as a strategy to camouflage his incompetence.

My head of school was a complete fraud. In speeches, she would tout her MBA and boast about her business savviness, but it didn't take much to uncover that she had no idea what she was talking about. In meetings, she would make references to research and curriculum that were fundamentally wrong. She wasn't even able to work her computer. She hired a full-time project manager amidst a budget crisis to do her PowerPoints, and projects, and serve as her henchman. It was actually kinda pathetic to watch. —*Teacher*

My bully was the same person who had put me forward for the job, and I was later to discover that she had set me up to "fail" (be a scapegoat for everything she had messed up) before my first day there. She was totally out of her depth in her role and under-qualified. In the two months before I started, she had incorrectly set up software, filed accounts for the company without understanding what she'd done, and buried tax errors. She was completely aware of her shortcomings but hid them by attacking and blaming others. —*Finance Manager*

Grandiose Yet Insecure

The Dragon is an intriguing mix of an overinflated sense of self and a deep-seated insecurity. His grandiosity makes him feel entitled to special treatment, and his "what's in it for me" attitude squelches any feeling of remorse as he steps over the bodies of his victims on the way to the awards podium, claiming ownership for work he hijacked or stole. Adept at playing the part, he often ingratiates himself initially to the Creative as a tactic to convince her to lower her defenses and divulge personal information that he will later use against her in the bully war.

I suffered needlessly due to a jealous, controlling, manipulative and narcissistic coworker who wanted credit, control and power. —*Fitness Instructor*

My manager was much younger and anxious about having to step in between to mediate. I did speak with him, but did not trust his ability to hold a professional space, as he often gossiped about other vessel managers. —*Shipman*

I feel harassment is predominant in the workforce. Staff that harass often are mentally unstable themselves or they feel threatened by workers who are more competent than they are. A lot of harassment is driven by their own jealousies, insecurities and behavioral issues.

They try to target the good workers and decent people in order to bring them down. I have seen so many staff that are getting paid good money who are old enough to know better, in their late forties or fifties, who spend most of their day at work scheming and trying to cause trouble for others. —*Government Administrator*

My boss is very manipulative, narcissistic and doesn't ever thank anyone for the progress or work done. Anything I do successfully is quickly forgotten, and then I get blamed for anything that goes wrong. —*Corporate Salesman*

Micromanaging

The Dragon's thirst for power is rarely quenched. In order to maintain her control, she often micromanages her underlings, barking orders for complex projects she does not understand. Her constant vigilance squelches creativity and disempowers employees.

> When I moved from my first district to my new district, there were all kinds of rules about how you have to do things that stifled creativity. I have had eleven principals in eighteen years. Some principals operate from a base of fear, and others have the ability to work around such structures. Although teaching can be very isolating, "close the door and nobody knows what you're up to," this new micromanaging has changed the culture and driven innovative teaching underground. —*Teacher*

> I was isolated from decision makers when I pointed out flaws and inappropriate conduct. I was submitted to nonstop micromanagement and draconian time-keeping schedules requiring me to report where I was every fifteen minutes. I was ridiculed and humiliated as my superior locked my ability to move into a different department and demanded that I meet with her constantly because she was the "only one" who could help me get better. —*Computer Analyst*

Jealous

The Creative often conceptualizes power as "power within," aspiring to grow up and out from yesterday's version of herself. In other words, she is on an inner journey of development and redemption, and though that work may be influenced by her outside environment and relationships, it is not dependent on them. The Dragon is quite the opposite; she thinks about power in terms of "power over," and this lens of the world incites her immeasurable rage when others pass her on the ladder up, provoking fierce feelings of jealousy.

> I was constantly being bullied because they thought that I was going to get the big job before them. So, they decided to hurt me in every way possible by talking about me and making false accusations that caused me mental grief and eventually a PTSD diagnosis. —*Mortgage Broker*

> Unfortunately, my success did not please everyone as the Dean was incompetent and jealousy was aroused, so I ended up becoming denigrated. —*Professor*

> I was a tenured Associate Professor. My publications were the most prestigious in the department. I was a member of the Faculty Senate and prominent in community service. Then one semester a powerful male member of the department orchestrated a bullying campaign against me. While the other department members picked the courses they would teach, I was assigned the worst courses and stepped all over. —*Professor*

Unethical

The Creative arrives on Mother Earth with an innate sense of decency. He feels twinges of uneasiness when he witnesses others teetering on the ethical tightrope and is spurred to speak up for justice, even when it comes at some cost to him. The Dragon, unfortunately, walks boldly on the paths marked "win at all cost" and "cover your tracks," actions that are hard to contest, for she experiences little remorse for damages done.

> Over the course of a year I became increasingly aware of how she was disrupting the office and trying to manipulate me into making decisions that suited her. If I made a decision that she didn't like, she would either sabotage me, or raise a complaint about me with my manager, who would force me to overturn my decision. —*Government Worker*

> The nurse manager put falsified personnel reports in my file. Another time she changed something on a patient's file the doctor had written. When I reported her, I became the one under attack and scrutiny. —*Nurse*

> The Headmaster would make up lies about different employees he wanted to get rid of. Then he would drop innuendos about them in meetings, slowly destroying their reputation. He wanted only yes men. If you had a degree higher than his or a knowledge base he found threatening, you were not chosen for committees or leadership positions at the school. —*Teacher*

In summary, the Dragon often is hired for her grandiosity, yet she lacks the necessary skills and social competence to handle the job. She defaults to status quo thinking and maintains power through micromanagement. When others steal the spotlight, jealousy overcomes her, triggering attack mode. Guided by power instead of mission, she often pushes ethics to the side, dealing in closed-door conversations, avoiding the light of transparency.

Next, you will meet the Shapeshifters, the Community Builders, and then the Figureheads, who all play pivotal roles in the bully war. Last, you will be introduced to the Leader. Hail the unicorn, the Creative's hope for a transformational partner on the job.

THE SHAPESHIFTERS

> The Shapeshifters yearn for recognition, sautéed in the need for power, the word "Control" tattooed on their upper thighs, a secret identity of aspiration. Lacking the fortitude of the Dragon, they clip to her cape, riding alongside her highway of mayhem. Deep-seated fears of unbelonging flood their bloodstreams, fully willing to break all ethical codes in order not to disappear.

The Shapeshifters are hollowed, empty of independent thought. All that remains is a burning desire to stand in the winner's circle or sit at the podium banging a gavel, determining others' fates. For Shapeshifters, however, this is a distant dream, for they lack the confidence of the Dragon, so they hang onto her scales and transform into anything she needs to get the job done. Their power, in this sense, comes from proximity; simply being near the puppet master makes them feel privileged and important. Their desire to maintain their position at the table makes them willing to commit unspeakable acts, for they lost their honor decades back and now have no semblance of decency left.

The Dragon recognizes the power she has over the Shapeshifters and uses them to do her dirty dealings, keeping her claws clean. She insists that her plans are carried out with precision, dictating each step, yet smiling at the Creative as they pass in the hall, fully knowing the demise that awaits him.

In order to ensure against a coup, in which the Shapeshifters attempt to usurp her power, the Dragon tracks their moves, controls their conversations, and dictates their relationships. Once in a while, as a reminder of her dominance, the Dragon will strike a Shapeshifter, expelling him from the lair, making him beg to reenter.

Shapeshifters are ever-changing, making them difficult to spot. They may be the cordial colleague asking the Creative for coffee one day, the plant in Human Resources spinning tales the next, and then the following day found busying their afternoon by falsifying records in an effort to seal the Creative's dismissal. Often the Creative is on the lookout for the Dragon, but it is the Shapeshifters who will likely sign her exit ticket.

The nurse manager bully gave her friends a balanced schedule during the day, leaving me short staffed at nights. She constantly would consult her followers and make them do the dirty work, so she didn't get in trouble with the higher ups or unions. When I would reach out to them for help, appealing to their compassion, they just laughed at me. —*Nurse*

My supervisor would not talk to me. Her body language was completely closed off in morning meetings. I would ask her directly how we could make things easier between us and she would just smile and walk away. The other workers did everything she asked, constantly seeking her approval. They were of course awful, to me because that is what she told me to do. —*Massage Therapist*

My supervisor hired a new manager for our group. My supervisor and manager became best friends, and started eating lunch together and getting together after work. The more time I spent with the new manager, the more I learned she was superficial and not truthful, traits that go against my core values. We would have meetings and she said things that weren't true, presenting erroneous information. Yet, this went totally unnoticed or unwilling to be noticed by my supervisor. —*Nurse*

My boss managed to install two other friends in the office in a different department, and I noticed a horrible shift. Less people chatted to me, conversations would stop when I walked in the room. At the same time, my co-worker left and her replacement also came via my bully.
—*Finance Manager*

My Assistant Principal presented herself like we were friends, always pumping me for information and whispering gossip in my ear. Over time, I let my guard down and began to trust her. Little did I know she was collecting intel on me to give to the Superintendent, who was intimidated by my high ratings and success record. He feared I was coming for his job, which I wasn't. Over a couple of years, my Assistant Principal filled my head with lies, made me weary of people I later found out were kind and trust-worthy, and gave me terrible advice, secretly dictated by the superintendent, in a secret plan to get me out. It worked. I lost my job, but now I am thankful to be out of such a toxic environment. I am frustrated with myself for trusting that woman. The Assistant Principal is now doing the same thing to the new principal. I know she is deeply insecure and a little pathetic. —*Principal*

COMMUNITY BUILDER

Smooth waters, sailing lightly, conscious not to make a wake. Silent smiles shared across the hallway, subtle messages of shared support even amidst internal trepidation over what is transpiring. As the guillotine is erected, assuring the Creative's pending demise, she swallows her dissent, nodding in agreement as the soldiers proclaim full community support for the execution.

Community Builders are inherently good; they crave harmony and work hard to bring people together. They understand the hidden curriculum and are happy to oblige, meeting requests with a willing smile, even amid internal trepidation. Community Builders follow the path of least resistance, for they prefer not to cause a ruckus. Like Creatives, Community Builders have complex inner conversations as they grapple with how to contribute. Their "go-along-to-get-along" demeanor, however, makes them reluctant to speak out, fretful to cause discord.

This propensity to reserve their opinion makes them attractive to the Dragon, who is eager to use her dominance to sway public opinion. The Dragon quickly ingratiates herself to the Community

Builders, pulling them to the dark side before they know they have been captured. Once under the Dragon's spell, Community Builders often drift further and further inside themselves, keeping their concerns hidden, presenting a composed, united front to colleagues.

When a Dragon targets a Creative, a Community Builder will often try to comfort the Creative in the privacy of a one-on-one meeting but won't offer public support for fear of being targeted next. Once the bullying war intensifies, and the Dragon insists on the Creative's complete obliteration and ostracization, Community Builders usually go along with the mudslinging.

In contrast, in transformative organizations that slay the Dragon, the Community Builders, over time, with encouragement from the Creative, will engage in innovative work and show their light to the world.

> When I first arrived to my company, I had a guy I often partnered with on projects, and sometimes we would even go out for drinks. I thought we were friends. We even had his family and kids over to dinner. When the bullying started, I noticed he slowly drifted away. At the end, he wouldn't return my text or even acknowledge me in the hall. I know he was scared he would be targeted if people thought we were friends, but I wish he would have at least told me that. It is hard to be completely shut out overnight. —*Engineer*

> My school was very political, and there was a group of mean girls who really ruled the roost. Luckily, I met a friend who I thought I could trust and confide in. During our breaks, we would walk around campus or talk in our rooms about all of the craziness that went on and how we would change things. We were so alike in so many ways. Or so I thought. Once I decided to start speaking up about some of my ideas, I became a target of bullying. In a matter of a week, this person who I thought was my friend completely ghosted me. She wouldn't return emails, or texts, or sit with me in meetings. It really hurts to have someone turn their back on you. —*Educator*

FIGUREHEADS AND LEADERS

Figurehead sits at her desk, straightening the tilting tower of business cards, impressed by the letters that follow her name, unconcerned for the names that follow her. Pointing to her place on the hierarchy, she looks up, committing to memory the ones who matter.

The Leader aspires to leave a glittering in the dark corner, a new twist to the knot to establish a different hold. She reclaims materials and mixes new colors of paint, opening herself up to wild possibilities. Always scaling the wall, undeterred by the fear of falling, she is aware of her wings.

The Dragon is often in a leadership position but not necessarily on top. She may report to a head, a board, or a CEO who falls into the role of either Figurehead or Leader. Within this dynamic, a Dragon's preferred tools of gossip, intimidation, sabotage, and exclusion are rendered ineffective, so she is left with the sole weapon of manipulation—which she wields masterfully.

Although the Dragon orchestrates the manipulation, it is carried out by her Shapeshifters. In contrast, the Figurehead and Leader require direct contact. That change in dynamics calls for an alteration in her approach, one that may be stealthily sexualized, in which the Dragon plays subservient to her superior, making him feel desired, attractive, and powerful.

These tools prove alarmingly effective with the Figurehead, who is often quietly enraged by creativity's looming threat to his power and status. Within this relationship, the Figurehead becomes susceptible to the Dragon's innuendos of what he should do and who he should trust. In this compromised state, the Figurehead unknowingly transforms into a Shapeshifter, who dutifully carries out the Dragon's requests.

The Leader, on the other hand, sits in an open office that invites the spontaneous, steady input of others. This expansion leaves no room for private Dragon meetings, and the buzz of conversations from diverse voices disrupts the silence the Dragon's rule requires.

When the integrity of the Creative can no longer stand the Dragon's destruction, she will often break rank with the hierarchy and leap over the Dragon's authority to seek the support of her boss's boss. Tragically, meeting with the Figurehead will bring no solace or hope, for her reckonings will unearth primal insecurities that he has fought against angrily—the most salient that he is not smart enough, good enough, or respected enough to be in the position he holds, for if he were, he would have recognized the problem long ago.

In an effort to quiet the alarm bells, the Figurehead repudiates the complaints, seeks out the Dragon for advice in dealing with the disruption, and "together" they decide that the Creative is a trouble-maker who must be discredited and dismissed. The Figurehead's decision to turn on one of his most valued and innovative employees is easy for him to make, for the Dragon has quietly mixed poison into the soup she feeds his ego over private lunches.

If the coup is foiled, and the Creative manages to stay, her tenure is likely limited, for over time, she will become frustrated by the Figurehead's unwillingness to engage in critical conversations about the toxicity directing the company's cultures. In addition, institutions led by a Figurehead tend to be stagnant and stale, lacking the psychological safety, innovation, purpose, and transformational power the Creative requires to thrive.

However, if the Creative encounters a Leader when she goes to share her concerns about the Dragon, the Leader will listen intently, get curious about the problem, initiate a deep investigation, talk openly about the findings, and take swift action to counteract the injustices and pain brought by the Dragon's bully war.

The Leader, unfortunately, is a mystical, seldom-experienced phenomenon. Hail the unicorn. Leaders, unlike Figureheads, earn their position by disrupting systems in search of solutions to problems, tying their self-worth to ingenuity and progress, not a desire to be revered and possess power.

The Leader understands that autonomy, diverse perspectives, and dissent are powerful change mechanisms needed to break through mediocrity, fight status quo thinking, and create communities that are inclusive, kind, and competitive in global markets.

The Leader, unlike the Figurehead, personally engages in creative work and makes space so others can rewire the system without fear of rebuke, eliminating hierarchical structures that prove limiting. This type of environment nourishes the Creative's spirit, eliciting her loyalty and charging her to enact transformative change. The Dragon, however, is unable to exist amid the crumbled hierarchy, and thus likely will leave in search of a Figurehead who is susceptible to her manipulation and charm. If a Dragon stays, the Leader will strip her of her power and make her job security dependent on the humane treatment of others, the abandonment of her evil tricks, and the disbanding of the attack mob.

We had a woman in our department that terrorized me and my colleagues. She spread vicious rumors of affairs and wrongdoing in order to discredit anyone who got in her way. When she was with our Dean or Chair, she would stroke their egos and make them feel wanted and powerful. Over countless meetings, she fed them lies about me and so many others. By the time I reached out to them to complain, my reputation was shattered. I had six meetings with my Dean and each time he dismissed the problem as a personality conflict. Eventually, I had to leave, because I just couldn't take the torture anymore. She made me physically and emotionally sick. It took years and lots of therapy before I felt like myself again. When I left, instead of looking into my departure, my Dean hurried me out the door. He was later promoted. Unfortunately, my university likes to promote "yes" men who guard the status quo. I am so glad to be out of that place. I hear it is still in shambles. —*Professor*

Before my original supervisor retired, I would have characterized the work environment as healthy and innovative. I worked independently for the most part, but he was available to support me or help if I had questions. He also had a high level of expertise in an area where I was not as strong, so I was able to use him as a resource to get better. There was always an incredibly interesting case I was working on, and collaborated with other disciplines. I was constantly looking for better ways to do things or addressing novel problems. —*Psychologist*

During the dissertation phase of my Ph.D., my committee ganged up on me because they didn't like my Dissertation Chair. They were threatened by her confidence and high level of expertise. At my preliminary exams, they threw my paper across the table saying, 'That's not how we do things at this university.' They then went on to make comments that made it clear they didn't even read it. My Chair had enough. She stood up, took my hand, and walked me out of the room. She returned and told the tenured professors that they will never treat a student with such disrespect again. They continued to go after her and me, but she held her head high and kept doing her innovative work. They were so angry that they couldn't intimidate her. She taught me the power of standing in your integrity and convictions and, most importantly, taking care of your students. Unfortunately, you don't find many people like that in academia. She was a unicorn. —*Doctoral Student*

CONCLUSION

Creatives question and innovate. Dragons are the bullies. Shape-shifters carry out the crimes and start the fires. Community Builders pretend they didn't see the security footage and don't feel the heat. Figureheads act like there is no war. Leaders walk into the battle, stop the Dragon, and everybody wins.

In the next chapter, we will explore the settings where these characters play.

INVITATION #2

Reflect on the six characters described in this chapter and write who in your story fits the descriptions. Notice: Do people morph across characters as the bullying cycle progresses? Is it helpful to identify the characters in your narrative driving the script? Do other characters, not discussed in this chapter, emerge? Sometimes drawing visuals of each character in your play, with lines detailing their characteristics and actions, can be helpful in understanding how your plot unfolded.

Chapter 2

The Setting of the Battlefield

STAGE CREW

The stage has been set. The performance is about to begin. Actors take your places. Stage Crew, this play is largely about you. You create the scenery. Your handy work is the backdrop that drives this production.

Bullying, at its core, is not the result of a single individual wreaking havoc on a random employee; to the contrary, bullying is birthed inside a toxic culture that breeds and feeds destructive behavior, such as gossip, manipulation, sabotage, exclusion, gaslighting, and ostracizing with the predetermined goal to permanently drive out the Creative. It is a type of premeditated, well-orchestrated psychological violence perpetrated by someone with more power over someone with less power, be it hierarchical or social, with devastating physical and emotional consequences—including but not limited to high blood pressure, gastrointestinal issues, migraines, anxiety, depression, and at the worst of times, suicide.

The rules of engagement at such institutions—whether they be schools, universities, hospitals, corporations, government agencies, or nonprofits—cannot be found in the employee handbook, yet they are well understood, internalized, and closely followed by those who work there. The toxic nature of such cultures is well known throughout the institution and surrounding community, often carefully hidden by a veneer of forced positivity and niceties one centimeter thick.

So, although each toxic culture has its own brand of destruction, most exhibit some or all of the following eight practices that emerged from my data. Intermixed with the descriptions, you will hear the voices of the brave Creatives who boldly told their stories of navigating land mines at work.

STRICT HIERARCHY

Cultures ripe for bullying depend on gatekeepers who guard the status quo, monitor collaborations, and control the conversation. Such narrow lanes prevent the free flow of information, only allowing privileged and vetted discussions to transpire. In such environments, employees are discouraged from outside partnerships and prevented from talking with people above or below their level. In order to keep the reins tight, all meetings are carefully monitored, and only selected individuals are invited to serve on committees and projects with a high public profile. Those permitted to speak are selected based on seniority and demonstrated loyalty, not expertise, and are expected to stay on message, representing the collective and carefully curated voice of the organization.[1]

Over time, hierarchical barriers make employees reluctant to speak out, thus silencing their ideas and concerns. To overcome such obstacles, trust must be established among and between various levels.[2]

I left my position of twenty-four years due to bullying and abuse. I witnessed the bullying and abuse of my younger colleagues and peers by a Department Chair and Dean. It was possible to feel and mark the change of climate from one of professional collegiality to one of top down at my organization, because we lacked a union or functioning faculty senate. I held on until I could take retirement and then exited as quickly as possible. —*Professor*

HOMOGENEOUS THINKING

Diversity in thought, word, and deed brings myriad ideas enmeshed with possibilities and inherent questions. Inside this messy deconstruction innovation breathes, uncontained, the heterogeneity of it all welcoming each person's curiosity.[3] In toxic cultures, however, wonderings must be contained, because when they wiggle out of the box, they spur questions, placing a spotlight on what has been. Therefore, in an effort to limit speech and possibilities, cultures of control insist on normed thinking in which all employees are expected to subscribe to the same line of thought as those in power. This insistence on sameness squelches diversity, controls relationships, and ensures that originality is refused a seat at the board table.

My experience with being mobbed happened while managing a smaller volume women's clothing store. There was very little diversity in the clothing store and a supervisor belittled me for helping transgender customers. —*Fashion Assistant*

CONFLICT AVOIDANT

Control the message, limit the conversation, and insist that a good culture is a polite culture, and you just might begin to master conflict-avoidant communication. The problem is that inside such environments, employees internalize the message that it is more important to present a positive, cordial front than to tell the bold truth. Because as humans we are wired to express ourselves, over time this performance of niceties makes employees draw inside themselves and disengage from work.[4]

And the issue is not limited to work environments; research shows that partners who shy away from crucial conversations suffer lower immune responses.[5] So what are crucial conversations? Crucial conversations are exchanges where the stakes are high, emotions intensify, and the outcomes are formidable.[6] In the absence of these tough talks, political correctness can be used as a tool of repression, ensuring that people don't speak up, resulting in institutional problems multiplying over time as employee engagement plummets.

PC language was used in a way to punish people rather than ensure the workplace was safe. —*Development Officer*

During faculty meetings we open up by sharing professional and personal celebrations, then we go over managerial items that could easily be shared via email, and then dismiss. The culture is such that meetings are meant for positivity; there is no room to speak about hard topics that impact the Department. If someone is brave enough to bring up an issue, our Chair usually says we will need to hold off on that discussion for another time. It makes the meetings pointless and a time suck. It's bizarre, you have a room full of PhDs and all we do is clap and smile when we are together. The Department is in peril, but we are not allowed to discuss how mismanagement has led to our current state of affairs. —*Professor*

LACK OF CONSTRUCTIVE FEEDBACK

Feedback is food for improvement, and when garnered with compassion, expertise, and specificity, it opens us up to new possibilities. Often, we live inside our own experiences, blind to how those around us interpret our actions and attitudes. Unfortunately, in bullying cultures, feedback is either nonexistent, exceptionally harsh, or lacks specificity. This conundrum is magnified for women, who research shows, receive 32 percent less feedback than their male counterparts, and the feedback they do receive, they struggle to act upon, because it is disproportionately focused on their communication style instead of their work, or it is distressingly vague.[7] To amplify the problem, in toxic cultures when employees attempt to garner or clarify a critique, they are often met with silence or indeterminate utterances. Over time, this frustration causes employees to disengage from the workplace or seek new employment opportunities where they can grow.

She said "I come across as cold," yet she failed to embed her comment in context nor follow it with actionable steps to address the concern. I notice that the feedback women get tends to be couched in relationship dynamics such as communication styles, whereas men are given specific feedback on technical skills, which is easily measured and actionable like, "You should familiarize yourself with this new accounting software. It will allow you to do more complex analysis for your clients." —*Manager*

I turned in a grant application for peer review and received a response with no constructive criticism. I was simply told my work wasn't "endorsed" by the university. —*Researcher*

BLAME, SHAME, AND CASH IN

In blame, shame, and cash-in cultures, profits are placed above people, and curiosity remains dormant. When problems arise, instead of getting curious about what transpired, higher-ups select a scapegoat to pin the problem on and then exchange high fives as they bury the issue in the backyard. In such environments, employees are asked to swallow emotions such as uncertainty, anger, comparison, burnout, perfectionism, despair, and regret in exchange for big-ticket smiles on frozen faces.[8] In response to these Stepford wives' performances, employees go underground with the complexities of their emotional lives, leaving them disconnected at work, now only lugging half of themselves to the office.[9]

Such retreat has dire consequences because when employees don't feel seen, they are not willing to take intellectual risks and get comfortable being uncomfortable, both prerequisites for professional growth.[10] Moreover, the dearth of compassion makes the workplace feel unsafe, which is consequential, for research at Google found the most salient trait of successful teams was a sense of psychological safety.[11] In addition, this sense of danger prevents employees from taking in feedback, for high critique only works in cultures of high care.[12] Moreover, a focus on the bottom line, instead of employees' feelings and the organization's mission, results in attrition and disengagement.

> My boss was very supportive of "blue sky research," but my experience with the larger university, was that unless it would lead to income to the college, they did not care about it. —*Professor*

ALL-IN-THE-FAMILY HIRING

Often in hiring committees, members are in search of a "good fit," which equates to, "We want to find people who look and think like us." In moments of inspiration, teams will craft a position targeted at expanding their offerings and stretching their identity. In higher education, this may equate to a teacher education program searching for someone with an extensive trauma-informed care background; in marketing, it may play out as an advertising firm setting its sights on bringing aboard a colleague with more global experience and reach. However, what often happens is that when these new employees arrive, they are, well, *different*! And different scares the pants off of people.

Different looks like a principal hired to bring research-driven practices and compassion to an elementary school that has struggled to evolve, who looks at the young students under her care and questions whether the school's move to integrate a daily yoga practice to counteract the alarming number of children under psychiatric care for stress and anxiety is just a Band-Aid approach, failing to address the root of the problem. In search of answers, the principal eats lunch each day with the children, committed to coming to know them as people with hopes, needs, and wants. Inside those conversations, a salient theme starts to emerge. The students spend upward of four to five hours a day, staying up close to dawn, to complete their homework. This workload is on top of a seven-hour school day punctuated by after school activities. With this realization, the principal, who is a seasoned researcher, shares with the district leadership team that excessive homework in elementary grades shows negligible correlation to academic achievement.[13] Despite the research, the principal is attacked for her "lack of rigor," her contract is not renewed, and the following year she is replaced with "one of their own."

In universities, "one of their own" refers to people working in the same institution where they earned their degree. Though it can be beautiful and rewarding to give back to the community that raised you, it can become problematic when high numbers of graduates work for the college they attended, because it creates a tight inner circle, with narrow group norms, made up of insular ideas tied to a "we have always done it this way mentality."[14]

In other companies and nonprofits, all-in-the-family hiring may mean that the organization is composed in large part of family members, where loyalty is often to each other instead of the organization's stated mission. In such situations, individuals sometimes hold work titles based on who they are instead of their level of expertise, causing resentment within the organization and strife when job responsibilities are mishandled.[15]

I worked in a family practice where I was the only employee who was not a family member. Upon being hired, I immediately felt like an outsider. They made fun of my Ivy League degrees and denigrated my unique training and expertise. I was left out of work social events and often not invited to meetings where new policies and practices were discussed. —*Social Worker*

PEOPLE IN POWER LOOK THE OTHER WAY

Most Creatives possess what Janoff-Bulman refers to as a benevolent worldview, believing that the universe is kind and just, and when given the good-faith opportunity to right a wrong, management will attempt a course correction.[16] But what happens in that moment of bifurcation, when the Creative shares information with his medical director, board of governors, supervisor, or CEO that employees are hurting patients, harming students, degrading staff, or taking financial liberties with the company's assets?

Inside that moment, the whole is cracked into two, signifying the world before and after the whistle-blowing. Whistle-blowing, according to Near and Miceli, is the "disclosure by organization members (former or current) of illegal, immoral, or illegitimate practices under the control of their employers, to persons or organizations that may be able to effect action."[17] However, what do you do when the leaders who are now in the know do nothing? That is the prevailing experience of the Creative living and working in a toxic culture, likely due either to ethical fading, bad followers, and/or distributed moral authority.

Ethical fading is what happens when, over time, ethically fluid leadership creates a culture in which degrading coworkers, threatening colleagues, and covering up moral corruption is the norm, such that the marketing department becomes adept at spinning tales, and Human Resources become expert at nondisclosure agreements to protect the institution from liability.[18]

In order to keep the toxic culture breathing, organizations need a concerted group of bad followers who tend to fall into one of three categories. The first group, fearful of disrupting the power structure, thus acquiesces to appease management; the second group are Dragons-in-training who thrive on drama and discontent; and the last group are isolates, who just want to be left alone and can't be bothered with things such as truth and fairness. Solas puts it this way: "Bad leaders would not be able to realize their ambitions without the support of dedicated, opportunistic, docile, or indifferent followers. Their success is assured by the complicity of the silent majority. Going along with villainy certainly resolves the dilemma of self-sacrifice."[19]

Distributed moral authority, on the other hand, is a model of diffusion of responsibility in which each Figurehead the Creative reaches out to in search of support runs the "what's in it for me" internal calculations and defaults to inaction, leaving the cleaning staff to mop up the mess that the injustice caused.[20] This counterintuitive reaction is puzzling to whistle-blowers, who by nature tend to possess a passionate ethical identity and exemplify a high degree of moral courage, causing most to contend that blowing the whistle on bad behavior is less a job requirement and more a moral obligation, knowing fully that they likely will come under attack for what Devine and Maassarani refer to as "committing the truth."[21]

> The two men made a complaint about my teaching. I was subject to constant gossip and left out of meetings. When I complained, the Dean and Vice-President just told me to ignore the bully. That I was better than them. —*University Lecturer*

> After three years the company became so busy that more staff were taken on including in our department and that was when the tide turned. My bully was deeply threatened by the idea of a new person joining the team, someone she hadn't been involved in hiring, someone with qualifications she didn't have (but implied she did). She made the mistake of openly bullying my new co-worker from day one. My new co-worker was young and inexperienced but super bright, keen, helpful, and quick. She attempted to resign the day after she first met my bully, one week into the job, but was persuaded to stay. It was like the genie was out of the bottle, and an office full of people had seen my bully in action actively bullying someone, and my boss had witnessed it. Unfortunately, my boss did nothing. —*Finance Manager*

> Incompetent management would rather keep bully employees who are skilled at the job rather than listen to new employees not as skilled because this makes more work for the manager. —*Case Manager*

THE DRAGON STAYS AND BLOWS THINGS UP

I have stood witness to countless stories of workplace abuse, attempting to make a safe space for Creatives' testimonies, sometimes continents apart but brought together in the pages of a shared chapter that made us question the divine nature of things.

Across these tellings, an almost unanimous desire shone forth. The Creative wants justice, not so much in the monetary sense as in a public denunciation of the Dragon's wrongdoing, punctuated by the tormentor's dismissal. In a scene from a just and hopeful world, the Creative regenerates her faith in the organization after witnessing its commitment to establishing a healthy working environment built on the ethics of human care.

Unfortunately, when it comes to workplace abuse, such a scene rarely transpires. The majority of Creatives lose their job while the Dragon suffers few to no consequences; some even are promoted as they move on to their next victim. A common tactic in the unfolding of this upside-down fairytale is for the Dragon to orchestrate chaos to divert the public's attention from her actions and, in many cases, her lack of content expertise. In the concocted whirlwind, the people get wrapped up in the manufactured crisis instead of recognizing that a star employee just walked out the door.[22]

An excerpt from the Dragon's Chaos-Making Manual:

1. Manufacture a crisis such as a security breach, a failed campaign, or an untapped market the competition is about to seize.
2. Blame the Creative. It is her fault that the capital campaign failed, the school is in distress, the market tanked and investors are calling foul, and the organization's most lucrative client bailed.
3. As you set off the fire alarm and scream emergency, search the Creative's work files for solutions. After all, she was the one with an innovative mind-set, diligent work habits, and record of program success.
4. Steal the Creative's work, pass it off as your own, and get busy solving the crisis you created as Human Resources and the legal team push the Creative out the door and assure her silence with a nondisclosure agreement.
5. File the NDA next to the others and destroy the security camera footage that stores the truth.

I did the work better than she could and was much more of an asset (productivity and expertise-wise, not politically, I guess) than she is. And they loved me. Now things are in shambles, people are worried, and everyone in the department is miserable and desperate to quit.
—*Clinical Psychologist*

She was so deeply insecure about her incompetence and wrapped up in her image, she went after anyone that threatened her power. It was usually the smartest hire she tried to get rid of. To do the job, she made up lies like the person stole computer files or got a DUI. Then when the gossip got going, she would quietly push them out the door, quickly replacing them with a person who she knew she could control. She has totally tanked the department with her poor leadership. —*Teacher*

CONCLUSION

Bullying, at its core, is not about the Dragon but the setting that enables the Dragon to thrive. Though the Dragon weaves in and out of the professional world, she only settles in institutions with a scenario that supports her story. Inflexible in her manner and approach, the Dragon requires a certain type of staging to survive. A strict hierarchy is a must, for it ensures that she remains atop the institution's organizational job chart. In order to dissuade questioning that may shine a spotlight on her mismanagement and lack of expertise, she insists on homogenous conversations, in which a single plotline that she sets prevails.

When problems arise, instead of getting curious about the cause, the Dragon digs a hole, places the conflict inside, and plants flowers on the freshly shoveled dirt, creating a temporary illusion of beauty and success, even as the roots are rotting. When it becomes impossible to cover up the mistakes, the Dragon identifies a Creative she can blame and shame while simultaneously enjoying the payouts from her profit sharing. One strategy she uses to keep the Creative at bay is hiring those who are already devoted subjects, valuing loyalty and family ties above expertise. To protect her position, the Dragon ensures that she is surrounded by Figureheads who can be easily manipulated and controlled. Always engaged in a battle for power, the Dragon devotes her time to denigrating and dismissing the Creative who threatens her reign. If such a strategy is not initially successful, the Dragon creates a cloud of chaos so nobody notices the Creative shouting fire while fleeing the premises.

INVITATION #3

Reflect on the setting where your bullying took place. Using the characteristics discussed in this chapter, describe the setting as if you were writing a novel and creating a vivid picture for the reader about where the story transpired. You may find it helpful to draw a picture of the setting, highlighting various characteristics and labeling pertinent places where the abuse unfolded.

Chapter 3

The Plotlines that Drive the Conflict

WHEN THEY SAY THAT, THEY MEAN THIS

I wanted to follow up with you today about some concerns that were brought forth by a colleague. Sincerely, *Human Resources*

Because your work is superior, and we have no grounds for termination, we have concocted a false complaint by an unnamed source and used this invisible man as a power pawn in our plan to start the paper trail necessary to kick you out on cause, therefore avoiding litigation or the threat of an expensive buyout. Sincerely, *The Inhumane and Not Resourceful Department*

I am sorry I am not able to go to lunch with you today, but I have another obligation I must attend to. Sincerely, *Vern*

It has come to my attention that the Dragon wants you gone. In order not to be targeted next, I am going to limit opportunities for us to be seen together. It will begin by canceling our weekly lunches, progress into not returning your texts, and culminate with me joining ranks with the oppressors, testifying that I never really liked you anyway. Sincerely, *Your Fair-Weather Friend*

Because we value you as an employee and want to help you move on to your next chapter, we would like to offer you this severance package. To indicate your agreement, please sign here. Sincerely, *The Company Lawyers*

The stories you have told us, partnered with the emails you have saved, put us at great risk for a lawsuit and a public relations nightmare. In order to avoid facing our institutional problems and the consequences of our unethical behavior, we are offering you a small

severance, which may cover tonight's dinner, in exchange for you signing this nondisclosure agreement, thus silencing your story forever.
Sincerely, *Department of Intimidation and Cover-Ups*

In workplace abuse, a universal story involves an entanglement
of plotlines that reproduce across people's tellings. As a narrative
inquiry researcher, when I interview victims of workplace bullying,
I simply say, "Tell me your story" and then hold space for what they
have to share. As I listen inside that sacred space, they often say,
"You won't believe what happened next." But I do believe it, and in
most cases, though I don't know the specifics of what they are about
to share, I can almost always predict the general plotlines.

My predictive powers are not predicated on a psychic gift. They are
an outgrowth of hearing hundreds of stories from victims across the
United States, Canada, England, Germany, Netherlands, Scotland, Australia, New Zealand, South Africa, and India. And what I have found,
and research supports, is a predicative cycle when emotional terror
shows up on the job. This is a good thing, because what can be predicted can be identified, and what can be identified can be prevented.

Because I am a storyteller at heart, in this chapter we will look at
workplace abuse through the framework of several story lines, providing a variety of entry points to understand the bully narrative's
unfolding. I will begin by revisiting chapter 2's discussion of Joseph
Campbell's monomyth, or the hero's journey, and then offer a fantastical retelling of the monomyth situated in the bully's war. Next,
I will share a multigenre depiction through consecutive daybook
or journal entries created as a composite case study. Then, you will
meet Jane, a blended case study depicting a typical bully war and,
lastly, a description of workplace abuse will be told as a six-act play.

THE HERO'S JOURNEY

The story of the human experience is a shared narrative of wanting,
hurting, and overcoming the turmoil of a world that often quakes
with anger and indifference in our quest for transformation, be it
individual or community centered.

As introduced in chapter 2's descriptions of the characters of
workplace abuse, Joseph's Campbell's monomyth provides a story
arc of venturing into the unknown in search of insight.[1]

Using some of Campbell's primary characters, let's do a brief overview of the hero's journey.

According to Campbell, the monomyth initiates within the hero's everyday experience, providing insight into her disposition and relationships within her ordinary world. Next, is a call to the extraordinary, an adventure the hero initially declines but eventually embraces as she leaves the safety of the known and sets off to explore a new dimension outside her current conception of self. Upon entrance to this novel space, she receives guidance from mentors who attempt to prepare her to cross the threshold officially. In this alternate universe, she gains new skills by navigating tests and challenges, culminating in an epic battle where she claims the elixir. The journey concludes when the hero returns to her known world, armed with new insights and understandings to bestow on her community.

The monomyth, according to Campbell, is embedded in mythology and is present across cultural stories. Writers and directors continue to lean on its structure, as evident in J. K. Rowling's book *Harry Potter and the Sorcerer's Stone* and George Lucas's *Star Wars* franchise, which he worked in close consult with Joseph Campbell during its creation.[2]

THE CREATIVE'S CONUNDRUM: A FANTASTICAL RETELLING OF THE HERO'S JOURNEY

As a child, **HERo** senses the vibrational whispers of the imagination and recognizes her tool of curiosity. She walks forward boldly and inquires: Why? When? How? Her musings at first entertain and ignite the creative spirits of those around her as together they expand their views of the universe.

Over time, however, her peers put on their shirts labeled Expectations, lace up their shoes of the everyday, and strap on their backpacks to carry Conformity, preparing to get in line.

HERo refuses the invitation Compliance issues, wears purple instead of pink, and climbs a tree to watch her partner soldiers below complete their daily routine in unison.

Noticing her absence, Mediocrity grabs her combat boots and pulls her from the limb, demanding that she pack up her childish ways and quiet her imagination, stuffing her goblins and fairies back into the toy chest. Tragically, HERo acquiesces and relinquishes her true self, burying her, snuffed out and gasping for air.

Monotony fertilizes the grass beneath HERo's feet, and slowly the weeds wind through her laces. Forcefully grounded, HERo stands witness to her entanglement and knows she must break free or be enveloped by servitude to the single story.

HERo's initial maneuvers are met with resistance; she recognizes this pushback as their fear of Momentum. It is quite scary to step on the young grass of the prairie called Just Beyond, wide open and asking to be explored.

Despite her reservations, HERo charges toward Growth and Redemption, knowing that her story is so much more than the recycled plotlines the surrounding soldiers digest at breakfast, regurgitate at lunch, and feast on again for dinner. She opts out of that familiar yet ancient offering and breathes the unique air of her own lifeline, hoping it is enough to resist withering into extinction.

Inside HERo's early steps to discovery, **Mentor** enters stage left. HERo reminds Mentor of her younger self, recognizing her gift of storytelling. Hand in hand, they tour the lands, pausing periodically to discuss Mentor's sculptures placed atop mountains and in valleys. The sharing emboldens HERo to again question and create.

In this new land of inquiry, HERo meets **Herald**, who confirms the need for change. Herald's presence is fleeting; she wants to experience the momentum but has no intention of helping the forward motion; she simply does not have the stomach or stamina to construct a vision. Herald is a sign holder, not a change agent, and HERo senses that she cannot be trusted.

Prepared to enter the next stage of declaration, HERo takes the evening to rest. While lumbering, her legs lengthen, and Originality leaps out from its confines and dances about the room. As HERo wakes and once again feels whole, she finds her feet and grabs her rhythms, deciding bravely to accept her call to adventure.

Across days, months, and decades, HERo winds about, exploring her new neighborhoods, pulling back the standard-issue flowered wallpaper to reveal an infinite number of new stories, told to play small as they were held captive in the walls of control.

Compelled to free the hostages, HERo sharpens her skills, invites her courage, and swings her cape around her shoulders as she nods to the **Threshold Guardian**, who lounges across the doorway of the next realm HERo will enter.

HERo steps into her becoming.

She arrives different, a child of the fantasy world of possibilities; curiosity is intricately woven into her circuitry. Her unique wiring issues invitations for diverse ideas to gather for dinner and engage in conversations that nurture relationships many deemed impossible. Her spirit is found inside herself.

Shadow, passive in demeanor and void of voice, takes notice of her parties, hoping to be invited. Universe pulls out HERo's chair, and as she sits, all her "whys," collected in her childhood, flutter from her pockets and envelop the living room.

Shapeshifters watch from the sidelines, contemplating whether HERo offers influence and power. Shapeshifters encompass the form of an ally but will later hold the knife directed at HERo's heart. Shapeshifters are gutless, void of depth and integrity; they will change into anyone who will bestow upon them an empty title.

Threshold Guardian, still situated at the doorway, witnesses the commotion and sends word to **Dragon**, who idles in her office, running the metrics on her next proposal, gauging the audience's approval rating, careful not to innovate and disrupt.

Dragon is blind, visionless, and guided by her greed and thirst for power. Upon rising from her throne draped in recycled story lines, she descends on HERo, placing droplets of poison on HERo's fluttering "whys," eliminating all options of dissent.

Dragon is prepared to fight to preserve the single story that serves as the foundation of her influence and control. Dragon does not engage in direct combat but, instead, uses the coward's tools of manipulation, gossip, sabotage, and ostracization—each strategy implemented by Shapeshifters, who morph and change as they infiltrate the lands in search of their own validation of self while propelling the plots of the everyday.

Shapeshifters initiate the reputational infiltration over tea with the Shadows, small followers who delight in gossip and simplicities, their spines liquified years ago. Shadows long to be included and are quick to deflect any narratives that prompt them to reevaluate the deep mediocrity they settled into long ago.

As lunch concludes, Shadows pull out their chairs, mount their brooms, and whisk across campus, dropping innuendos, slowly sabotaging HERo's work and reputation. To deepen the hole, Dragon invites her own masters to supper and slyly suggests that HERo's success is attributed to Dragon-directed initiatives.

HERo, however, continues to create, not yet feeling the weight of her diminishing reputation as she slowly begins to sink. Once the new heaviness alerts HERo to her fall, she confronts Dragon and demands that the poison be siphoned away. Dragon, uninterested in purification, launches the cannons and proclaims victory.

Broken and hurt, HERo reaches for the Shapeshifters, but realizing that they can no longer ride her tattered cape, they turn and walk away, disappearing into the smallness of their resolve and perspective.

Committed to rising, HERo tips her hat to Threshold Guardian standing at Dragon's exit gate and walks into the next realm, charging her subplots to expand into eternity. Gathering beginnings, middles, and ends over infinity, HERo returns to the ordinary world with the elixir, in the form of the infinitude of stories, and those bold tellings eventually slay the Dragon.

She and we are free.

Below is a composite narrative, drawing upon themes that emerged across hundreds of case study plotlines, presented as daybook entries.

DAYBOOK ENTRIES: OFFICE LIFE

Boys draw in journals, and girls lament in diaries, but I will tell my story in a daybook, its pages bold like me.

August 6, 2021
Momentarily emboldened with a sense of pride, I stepped onto the soft pile rug of my new corner office, quizzically searching over my shoulder for sightings of the impostor police, for surely by now they have figured out I didn't earn the right to be here. Except, I did.

August 13, 2021
I hung three diplomas on my office walls, unphased by the mess I made as I attempted to get the spacing just right. I assume I am settling in for a long stay.

September 23, 2021
I am stepping softly and walking slowly this first year, almost like a ghost, floating, an anthropological excavation, listening, trying to understand this peculiar place. Already logged forty-five hours of lunchtime conversations and coffee chats, holding space for colleagues' celebrations, questions, and concerns. I'm not sure if anyone has ever pushed back the walls, making room for them to tell their story.

October 26, 2021
Seventy-four pages of notes, a research story of sorts, downloads of quaking in bathrooms to avoid the Dragon, and hash marks to track the covert attacks of a group of women who forgot this isn't high school. I am not so sure I belong here, but I feel I have something to wrap up and give, perhaps providing cracks of light for people who feel weighed down by the darkness, almost forgetting that it is sunny on the other side of the curtain. I see the potential in the corners, not growing enough to be seen. It is all so lonely in this place. Each time I feel a connection, there is a slipperiness about it, as if nothing is real enough to stick.

November 8, 2021
I am beginning to pull the knots, straighten out the strings, so I can see the narrative threads. That colleague I thought may one day become a good friend has too many sides to make her comfortable to sit with. I can't tell what side is real, or perhaps she has gotten so used to melting into shapes that fit the room that she has lost herself in all her reconfigurations. I watch her picking up droplets of gossip and drinking them in while siphoning just slightly more from people than they want to share.

November 29, 2021
The holiday was a welcome respite with family, but work whispers are just loud enough that they are always in the corner of my mind. I surrendered some mornings to coding my notes. The researcher part of me is always in my pockets. This world is too fascinating not to search for meaning. Themes of stagnation, toxicity, and fear bleed from my highlighter as I color-code what seems to be a bit of a well-spun web.

December 21, 2021
I feel like we are moving this elephant down the path. It is a slow go, but some people here crave innovation and are spilling brilliant ideas all over the conference room table. After nights of feeling overwhelmingly hopeless, I see a crack in the sidewalk and a small sprout peeking up.

January 7, 2022
We are making progress. The community we serve is invigorated by the positive momentum. Perhaps I can make this work.

February 12, 2022
Liz, my boss, came by my office last night right when I was leaving, the office was dark, and only the night crew were still checking off their to-do boxes. Uninvited, she strolled in, sat, and casually started sharing that at last night's gala the table chat was about me, sprinkling words such as "incompetence," "disappointment," "bad fit." I kept looking for the escape door. I was craving feet-up time with my new novel, not a covert attack. I have only received positive feedback from colleagues and the public, so her words seemed like a fabrication from her imaginary world.

February 20, 2022
As I walked down the hall this morning, Christie looked at the floor, making me feel invisible. At lunch, my noon lunch group ate at 11:30 a.m.; I guess I got left off the text. At 3 p.m., my administrative assistant said I was no longer needed at the 3:30 board meeting—the meeting I called to discuss the new proposal.

February 28, 2022
Lonny in Human Resources sent me an email saying she wanted to discuss why I skipped today's meeting and a list of concerns my boss is sharing. I can see the ambush brewing.

March 15, 2022
I can't stay here. My heart told me that a month ago, but I tried to ignore it, pretending not to hear the conversations it was having with my gut. Now my migraines are getting louder, pushing me toward the door marked "Exit, No Reentry."

March 18, 2022
The proposal I spent the past six weeks on has mysteriously disappeared from my computer. The emails I marked "important," evidence of the abuse, have vanished from the server. The things on my desk are telling me they have been touched.

March 20, 2022
I worked on my resignation letter last night. A fog pulled back as I allowed myself to see new possibilities. Maybe my name badge is not my identity.

March 21, 2022
Before I wrote good-bye in the cement, I made an appointment to meet with Mike, Liz's boss, hoping he could hear my concerns regarding my experience and my worries for a department that was once again surrendering to the quicksand. His response was stale, clearly pre-stirred from strategy sessions with Liz. I should have known that she preempted my narrative months ago, towering over him with her heels. He is too concerned with keeping up appearances to question her plotlines—a typical Figurehead, blinders tight, content to let me drown if it allows him to keep his shined shoes dry.

March 27, 2022
The email is sent, my gut whispers to my lungs that it is safe to breathe, producing an unmistakable sign of relief. Already, I have two dinner interviews set up next week. I have asked to stay through the end of the fiscal year, providing me time to wrap up as many loose ends that allow to be tidied.

March 28, 2022
I arrive at work at 6:30 a.m., craving the moments before the office starts to bustle with conversations that no longer include me. I have accepted my ostracization. To take away someone's belonging is the cruelest of thefts.

April 2, 2022
Two emails on my personal account. Both interviews have been canceled. They no longer need to talk. The ostracization has bled outside the compound's walls.

April 6, 2022
This morning my security card didn't work, and I am no longer receiving company email. My cancellation is complete.

April 10, 2022
A phone call arrives at 11 a.m. sharing that I can retrieve my belongings at Security. All that remains of me are holes on the walls where my diplomas once settled, thinking they would stay.

MEET JUNE

June thinks past the corporate handbook and the hidden curriculum of how it should be done and inquires, "What if we tried it this way instead?" Her thoughts expand, invigorating her colleagues as they, too, get excited about the possibilities. June's peers pick her brain over lunch about what to do on the Jones account.

One of the VPs invites her to share her project idea at the upcoming board meeting. This is not unusual. June has been at the company for seventeen years, and colleagues lean on her for support, appreciating her genuine devotion to the work, kind demeanor, and what sometimes seems like a bottomless pit of passion and ideas. She makes people feel energized and alive, a reminder of why they got into this work in the first place.

The landscape, however, is changing.

Following an aggressive battle with cancer, her longtime boss decides that it is time to pass the torch, pack his office, and head west to breathe in the beauty of the desert with his family.

June is offered his job, a puzzle piece fit according to colleagues, but she declines, knowing that it would put her on a train moving her away from the mountain where her heart beats.

Josh arrives, towering but with a foundation that makes her shake.

Colleagues continue to be energized by June, except for Josh, who quietly rages each time his spotlight shifts to her.

While Josh publicly celebrates June's ideas, he starts to drop pieces of gossip over coffee, neatly wrapping his remarks in concerns that go something like this: "I sure do like June, but a few of the managers don't think she has the research to back up that proposal. I wonder if we should help her quiet down for a spell, so she doesn't come under review?"

At this moment, Josh is leading the invisible army, inventing conversations and attributing them to people of influence. Over the next month, Josh increases his troops and reaches out to his superiors to express misgivings regarding June's work.

At first, Josh's bosses balk, surprised by the concern, for June is clearly a superstar, but Josh persists, pouring lies into the sweet tea they sip over lunch.

While strategically orchestrating June's termination, Josh outwardly assures June that they are good friends, encouraging June to divulge personal information Josh can later use against her in the court of public opinion.

One afternoon, Josh shares his concocted worries with Human Resources, the department June will later find to be neither human nor resourceful. June's file overflows with accolades from colleagues and community members, so the director of Human Resources is caught off guard by Josh's complaints. To push the conversation forward, Josh subtly threatens the HR director's job while assuring her that he is only looking out for "June's best interest."

Acquiescing to the pressure, HR agrees to put June on a performance improvement plan (PIP). June is devastated and confused by this new development and requests specifics regarding the concerns listed. With only his invisible army to back him, Josh has nothing to offer but silence and generalities.

As the weeks drag on, Josh increases the lunchtime gossip, encouraging colleagues to shun June to avoid becoming "part of the problem," sets unrealistic project deadlines, forgets to invite June to meetings, and then publicly berates her for not being there.

Now, when June sits down in the company cafeteria, the colleagues she once called friends pick up their trays and leave, nodding to Josh, the puppeteer, who now insists on June's complete isolation.

In the quiet of the evenings, once witnesses have gone home, Josh pops into June's office, intermittently offering praise and condemnation, causing June to question her reality. Nothing is ever what it seems in this place.

At June's annual physical, her doctor is alarmed by her heightened blood pressure, decrease in sleep, and uptick in migraines. Terror and dread now arrive like clockwork each morning June pulls into work.

As the abuse becomes untenable, June reaches out to Josh's boss to detail the attacks, but the watercooler has already been poisoned.

As June walks down the hall, colleagues pretend not to know her, gossip spreads around her, projects are routinely sabotaged, and a culture of toxicity and stagnation is now pervasive.

In deep despair, June tenders her resignation and packs up her office as Security stands suspiciously at the door.

From the side window, Josh watches June's departure and delights as the status quo returns, innovation is squelched, and a culture of fear pervades as people vow to color inside the lines.

Delighted by his successful mission, Josh notices the spotlight on Trevor and prints copies of his next battle plan.

WORKPLACE BULLYING: A SIX-ACT PLAY

As a narrative inquiry researcher, I think of daily life as a story. The story of workplace abuse, however, is shocking and disarming for the unexpecting Creative, because an introduction to this recurring plot cycle was not part of her coursework at school. Nevertheless, the story script is quite predictable, as exemplified in my own study and detailed over decades by a number of researchers.[3]

Now find your seat: *Psychological Terrorism at Work* is about to commence. It is a six-act play, fast-moving, with no time for intermission.

Stage #1—She Doesn't Belong Here: Target Identification

This first stage includes a seismic reader and a telescope, as the Dragon senses the ground shaking and attempts to zoom in on who is making the ruckus. This rabble-rouser may be doing nothing at all, outside of living her true self. This authentic way of being may present as a break from tradition, whether it be in how she looks, where she is from, or how she interacts in the world. Whatever is contributing to the ground's movement, the Dragon contends that the hierarchy is being flattened and the status quo is being placed under a microscope. Therefore, the Dragon opens her notebook labeled "War" and begins plans for elimination.

Stage #2—Let's Be Frenemies: Jealousy and Case Building

At this stage of the attack, the Creative is unaware that she has been targeted. Instead, she may be grateful for the attention and cordiality of the Dragon. This fire-breather may praise her ideas and projects publicly in meetings, then suggest an afternoon coffee to celebrate her accomplishments. Inside these one-on-one social encounters, the Creative finds what she first identifies as friendship, prompting her to be vulnerable, disclosing personal information about her family life and career aspirations. Little does the Creative know that the "friend" sitting across from her is not a confidant but a killer, busily collecting intel to use against her in a future war. For example, if the Creative loves and excels at writing, and this talent to express her thoughts on the page is garnering positive attention, taking the spotlight, the Dragon may later decide to remove all of her job responsibilities related to writing, citing it as a weakness and a challenge.

Stage #3—Blame Her: Precipitating Event

To wage war and not be seen as an aggressor initiating an unprovoked attack, the Dragon must grab onto an event, flip the narrative, and craft a new story line in which the unfolding signifies the Creative's mismatch for the job. The point of this tactic is to turn the tide, lobbing the first grenades of character assassination.

In this stage, colleagues are made to believe that the Creative represents a formidable threat to their job stability. In this sense, the precipitating event is not the reason for the bullying but simply a moment to grab onto to recruit bystanders. For example, a marketing manager may put forth a campaign that has captured the positive attention of clients. In response, the Dragon starts whispering at the watercooler that the campaign's success will drive funds away from other initiatives, resulting in job loss. Thus, colleagues the Creative once considered friends and allies start to push her out of the inner circle and sabotage her work to maintain their own job security.

However, if the colleagues were to recognize reality, it would be clearly evident that the campaign in question will instead help to put the firm on the map, upgrading and expanding professional paths for all.

Stage #4—Watch Your Back: The Underground Battle

The initial attacks are a slow rain, a mist that is almost indiscernible to those getting wet. The Dragon initiates the drizzle that will turn into a downpour by dropping nuggets of gossip cloaked in empathetic concern. It may sound something like this: "I really like Doris, but ever since she joined the school, I have noticed that her new ideas are making the administration uneasy. Already, I hear whispers that she is not a good fit. I hope she will fall in line, so that she doesn't get in trouble." Or, "Patrice is an excellent nurse, but I am concerned that she spends so much of her energy talking to patients. All of her time spent in hospital rooms is going to burn her out, and we will end up having to cover her shifts." Though these worry drops are invalid, not grounded in reality, they help to construct a narrative that the Creative does not belong here.

To seal the deal of the Creative's unbelonging, the Dragon often will initiate informal interviews, where she pops into colleagues' offices unannounced and starts asking leading questions such as, "Have you noticed how much everyone seems to dislike Doris?" Or, "Isn't it crazy how much time Patrice spends comforting patients?" The answers to these questions, however, only have one response; due to the power dynamic between the Dragon and her underlings, colleagues quickly relinquish their independent thoughts and agree wholeheartedly, giving the Dragon new ammo as people go on record supporting fiction as truth.

At this stage, it is not unusual for the Dragon to approach her boss, executive board members, and other people of influence to share her "deep concern" for the Creative, thus laying a foundation of an emerging narrative that the Creative is a bad fit and not up for the challenges of the job. These pre-meetings serve as documentation that the Dragon will later fall back on when she starts to insist on the Creative's termination.

Such tactics help to solidify the Dragon's false narrative and ensure the Dragon's job security, for when the attacks escalate, and out of desperation, the Creative reaches out to the Dragon's superiors for support and assistance, no room will be left for her story because they already will have swallowed the Dragon's fictional version in its entirety.

Stage #5—Kick It Up a Notch: Escalating Attacks and Mobbing

At this stage of the bully's war, the Creative comes to understand that she is under attack. Surprisingly, it may be her general practitioner who helps her to unearth the battle, questioning why her blood pressure is elevated, her migraines are intensifying, and her heart is fluttering in the most peculiar way, for her body is a truth teller, sensing injustices, abuse, and trauma before her mind is aware.

At this point in the battle plans, in order to accelerate the Creative's destruction, the Dragon will fully commit to the character assassination, regularly sabotaging her projects and presentations, "mistakenly" forgetting to invite her to social events, and insisting that colleagues enforce her complete ostracization or risk "becoming part of the problem" Therefore, fearing for their own career trajectory, bystanders abandon their intention to stand up and, instead, slip into warrior clothes, placing the Creative smack in the middle of the scope of their recently issued weapon.

After weeks of sitting alone in the cafeteria, struggling to complete projects without the necessary resources, and committing to keeping her head high despite the gossip flung her way, the Creative often will reach out again to the Dragon's superior and Human Resources for assistance. The response, however, likely will be underwhelming, as they dismiss her concern, having already bought the completed plot the Dragon was selling.

In addition, to deepen the wounds, instead of responding to cries of abuse, Human Resources may busily cover the Dragon's dirty doings by putting the Creative on a performance improvement plan (PIP), officially starting the documentation trail that will eventually culminate in the Creative's termination. For it is far easier to put the skeletons back in the closet and destroy the security cameras capturing truth, blaming it all on the explorer for prying, than it is to get curious about the transgressions unfolding on the ground at work, despite reams of emails and other documentation corroborating the Creative's story, a narrative that reads more like a psychological thriller than a typical day at work.

Stage #6: You Are Out of Here: Exits and Cover-Ups

Though time lines differ, after enduring prolonged degradation and abuse, 67 percent of Creatives lose their job, through no fault of their own, by quitting, being forced out, fired, or transferred.[4] Many are asked to sign a nondisclosure agreement in trade for a measly severance and letter of recommendation, thus forever silencing the Creative's story and inviting the toxic culture to spread in perpetuity. Such endings leave Creatives without insurance or a support network when they are the most vulnerable, hampering their ability to seek medical attention to address the emotional trauma and physical decline, all a direct result of the bullying.

To sharpen the blow, though the victim often has been silenced by signing the NDA, the organization will continue to engage in Orwellian "doublespeak," enabling members to shift the narrative and avoid culpability, responding to public concerns about the slaying of a beloved member of the community with catch phrases such as "I am not able to elaborate on her departure," or "I really wish we could say more, but it is a confidential Human Resources issue." Such vague retorts are purposely voiced to explain the Creative's abrupt departure, making people contemplate that perhaps her transgressions, not a toxic culture, prompted her to go.

As the first Creative exits, and a new one enters, the play is set on constant repeat as the terrorism continues indefinitely.

CONCLUSION

It is important to understand the trajectory of workplace abuse because what can be identified can be stopped. Bullying can be called out, bystanders can become upstanders, and creativity can thrive in the context of an organizational culture that insists on psychological safety on the job.

INVITATION #4

Reflect on your bullying experience. Using the headings below as a guide, describe the cycle of your abuse. Is it helpful to identify how your unique experience fits into the typical trajectory?

1. Target Identification
2. Jealousy and Case Building
3. Precipitating Event
4. The Underground Battle
5. Escalating Attacks and Mobbing
6. Exits and Cover-Ups

Chapter 4

The Tools of Destruction

TO THE WOMAN WHO ALWAYS WORE SANDALS TO WORK

I know that you talk to me via text because you can't risk them seeing us together. I see you turn your head back and laugh at my expense. I feel the hand you don't reach out to unscramble the layers of lies they tell about me. Your silence is deafening. Did you know that it wasn't the Dragon's claws that won the pain war? It was you, the one who would join me for toast and honey and now labels me invisible and tasteless.

The national news, on any given day, tells calamitous tales of individuals who lost their lives at the hands of another through drowning, firearms, sharp objects, or poison, to highlight just a few deadly weapons. For the tools available to squeeze the last breath out of another are innumerable, only limited by the imagination of the worst offenders.

Dragons in the workplace, on the other hand, must skate the noxious line, plotting complete destruction while keeping their hands clean, assuring the avoidance of any responsibility. They simply want their victims permanently debilitated, unable to contribute or retaliate, but usually not dead. After all, plausible deniability must be maintained, and as long as the victim is kept breathing, in the United States, unlike other countries that ensure dignity at work for all employees, it is completely legal, outside of protective class, to bully a colleague on the job.

Thus, to avoid culpability, the Dragon is relegated to a small bag of tricks that she recycles and reinvents. It is as if an underground conference is held annually where Dragons attend catchy sessions titled "Gossip Girls," "Bait and Belittle," "Crumble Their Character," and "Ice Them Out Until They Melt."

So, though the tools discussed below now appear quite commonplace to me, a by-product of listening to hundreds of stories of Creatives across the world who have suffered workplace bullying, at the time of my own workplace abuse experiences I was completely unaware of these weapons of war. Thus, I was flabbergasted by the actions of perceived professionals, and continued, to my own detriment, to make the most gracious assumptions about their egregious behavior and, thus, was not prepared or equipped to defend myself.

The twenty-two tools discussed below all emerged as common themes from the data, with the first eight used most universally. As a reminder, it is essential that workplace bullying not be conflated with personality conflicts, for workplace bullying is a dangerous, at times deadly assault on one's character and personhood, as a health information specialist shares:

> The risk manager of the facility became involved because she saw the bullying that was happening. She was so outraged she ended up quitting her position in an open board meeting, but not before someone pulled her brake lines apart under her car. I know it sounds crazy but it happened.

THE PRIMARY TOOLS IN THE DRAGON'S TOOLBOX

As you will soon see, initially most Dragons rely on eight primary tools to wield their destruction and maintain control: humiliation and belittlement, gossip, smear campaigns, exclusion, sabotage, gaslighting, ostracization, and retaliation.[1] However, as the bullying progresses and intensifies, Dragons get more aggressive and creative in their assault, as evident in the additional fifteen tools.

#1—Humiliation and Belittlement

Humiliation strips the Creative naked and leaves her in the town square to endure the gawking. Inside that moment of complete exposure, her confidence shrinks until it is almost indiscernible. Belittlement is Humiliation's close cousin, laughing and sneering while exchanging class notes scribbled with incriminating details meant to strip away pieces of the Creative's dignity until she disappears inside herself.

The Dragon's scales are riddled with insecurity, so she must squelch the confidence of others in order to feel strong. For the Dragon's strengths depend not on her expertise, capabilities, relationships, or ideas but on her ability to eliminate the competition. Because she can't compete on merit and skill, she tramples her victim's dignity until they no longer remain in the game.

> Coworker made snide remarks as I walked into a room such as, "It's about time you showed up." Or she would walk by me in the hallway and make remarks such as "Hi loser," followed by laughter. There was ALWAYS one or more person(s) with her when she made these remarks, so other people would laugh after the comment. I usually said nothing in return, or my remark was "Whatever." A final straw came when she said something to me as she walked past me (as we were going in opposite directions) and I turned around and followed her (into the changing room at the end of our work shift) and said, "I'm sorry I didn't understand you." —*Nurse*

> I remember inviting her to my office so we could figure out a way to fix our relationship. When she arrived, she brought another colleague. As they sat there, she said right to my face, "I don't like you and I will never like you." The other person just smirked. I wanted to cry but was able to swallow the tears. However, the pain still sits with me. —*Educator*

#2—Gossip

Inside the bully war, the truth holds no buoyancy. What keeps the Dragon afloat are the weeds of gossip, tightly intertwining the Creative's limbs, keeping him chained below the water as others float above, bonding over fairytales. What makes gossip so alluring is what my colleague and friend Dr. Laura Dzurec calls sticky stories that draw in Shapeshifters and Community Members, as they bond over the delicious drippings of another's hardships.[2] Such connection creates what researchers refer to as common enemy intimacy, in which people bond not through authentic conversation, shared values, or joint interest but through collective devotion to hating the same people.[3] Gossip, in this sense, is a false god, making people join a community that when exposed to the light, evaporates into oblivion, leaving them alone and self-loathing.

They use gossip and rumors—death by a thousand cuts, until I finally took leave. —*Teacher*

She went about sabotaging people's character who she saw as a threat. She would say things like, "_____ is sleeping with _____ and that's why she was promoted." Her intention was clearly to destroy my reputation with colleagues, not only in my department but in other departments as well. —*Professor*

My eighteen plus years working in the operating room are full of experiences of targeted manipulation, gossip, and sabotage incidents where bullies actively lied and or exaggerated about situations of others to gain control, make others look bad, or set someone up for failure. —*Nurse*

I said something that made a coworker mad. Two weeks later another coworker starts finding the smallest things to get me in trouble. I was written up for the first time in seventeen years. My coworkers would go through my desk when I was out on a house visit. I even left a hidden note that said happy hunting inside my desk and I was written up for being aggressive?! —*Social Worker*

I was very lucky that a number of people found the way I'd been treated awful and they let me know the things they had overheard. Things like my bully had fabricated a story about me having a history of mental health issues, which she'd been repeating for years; that I had a history of having affairs with people; that she'd thought I use to steal things; and that I'd pursued my boss's brother-in-law—she said she'd recognized the signs (I've met him once in the office). —*Finance Manager*

#3—Smear Campaign

A smear campaign is Gossip's more sophisticated cousin. Though their similarities are undeniable, smear campaigns are more organized in their destruction, relying less on Gossip's tactic of the watercooler's disjointed banter and more on establishing a paper trail in which the lies can live in perpetuity, the fables stacking up, until a full book rests on the desk of the director of Human Resources, demanding her to act. Perhaps a performance improvement plan (PIP) is in order or a mediation session in which the power imbalance leaves the Creative outside as his bully sits at the negotiating table dictating terms.

Typically, the smear campaign begins with a whisper of impropriety to establish the Creative as a deviant. Common narratives from my case studies include false accusations of stealing computer files, sharing trade secrets with the competition, lascivious behavior, or undercurrents of incompetence. These allegations will be inserted into an evaluation or in an email from HR requesting a discussion, and voilà, the written word validates the false claims whether or not future investigations prove otherwise.

In addition, the power dynamic of workplace abuse, where heads bully tails and HR reports to the Dragon, who writes the narrative, makes for an unwinnable war. Moreover, Figureheads often support the smear campaign as they direct HR to silence the dissenters in an attempt to deflect legal liability. After all, honesty and dignity hold little value for swine during an afternoon of mudslinging.

> Private investigators were hired to harass, stalk, defame and steal from me in order to cover-up the crimes and corruption and to prevent a lawsuit. —*Teacher*

> I had a performance evaluation that included four extra pages of lies about me, and my character, and my work ethic. —*Teacher Aide*

> In some ways, the bullying made me feel like a hologram of me had been created, it looked like me and sounded like me but wasn't me at all. The person my bully described, the person my boss bullied and encouraged others to bully too didn't exist. The real me was sitting at my desk doing my job. The hologram was the version they created somewhere else when I was being spoken about behind my back and lied about and blamed and accused. If the company closes its doors, it feels as if the hologram would disappear with it, and it feels like the real me could just maybe fully exist again. But it's not something I can count on, I live in hope! —*Finance Manager*

#4—Exclusion

One of the most effective ways for a Dragon to craft a narrative of the Creative's incompetence is to disinvite him from meetings, mistakenly of course, and then punish him for not being there. His absence will first be duly noted on minutes with an exasperated promise from the Dragon to "catch him up," and then again highlighted for the Figurehead, when he fails to deliver a deliverable that the Dragon forgot to mention needed to be delivered.

Another strategy is to change the regular after-work Tuesday drinks at the corner bar to Thursday dinners at the new café across town but not share the updated invite with the Creative. This accomplishes three important tasks: First, he feels pushed out of the inner circle. Second, he is not there to defend himself as his reputation is broken over the breaking of bread. Last, his notable absence provides the foundation for a new narrative that he does not value company community building and thus his eventual banishment is both deserved and legitimized.

Over time, as natural pack animals, the herd begins to view him as a damaged member of the team. Thus, they commit to pushing him out of the group to avoid becoming prey. It begins by not saving him a place in the cafeteria, continues by evading his greetings in the hallway, and progresses to walking the other way when they spot him at a large company gathering. This othering weakens the Creative's resolve and defenses, making him an easier mark for the Dragon's ultimate plan of elimination.

My male supervisor was the primary culprit, but he enlisted the help of other employees in ostracizing me, spreading rumors and gossip about me, and harassing me until I reached the point that this behavior prevented me from being able to complete my work. —*Immigration Officer*

They kept me out of meetings on messaging, so two other peers could control it. They invited folks from my team but literally would not share what times the meetings were taking place at a peer level. It went on for three years. —*Advocate*

The most recent event happened on a district-wide planning day. We were separated into groups by the subject we taught. I was with the two other teachers who always excluded me. I asked if I could help them with the unit they were creating, and they gave me the cold shoulder. So I sat on the other side of the room by myself for the rest of the afternoon and worked alone. I didn't tell administrators about the situation, because it seemed like such childish behavior. —*High School Teacher*

I began to withdraw and not share my efforts as freely; I admit I lost enthusiasm and suspect both my manager and my supervisor sensed this. They began to shut me out of important meetings. Everyone would be invited from my department but me. They would not share important pieces of information that I needed to complete my projects. All of this happened very gradually, but at each occurrence, this caused me great distress. —*Health-Care Worker*

#5—Sabotage

What do you do when you want to make the most competent, creative team member appear to be a farce? Well, if you can't win the game, cheat. Victims of workplace bullying are most often top performers, possessing high levels of expertise and an overabundance of neurons firing sparks of innovation.

In order to stop the inertia, the Dragon will simply alter the landscape. As evident from the snippets of victims' stories below, this often resembles a psychological thriller more than classroom clown antics.

Sabotage at work, at its core, is the purposeful deflation of another's success by stealing, breaking, or withdrawing the necessary relationships or resources required to complete a task. This could equate to the artistic software an advertising executive depends on mysteriously being deleted from her computer, a financial adviser's essential accounting numbers magically changing at 2 a.m. while he sleeps, or a manager's dinner reservations with the lucrative client at the trendy new restaurant canceled by an unidentified caller.

Sabotage gives the Dragon the upper hand by changing the rules, deleting the resources, severing the relationships, and then filming the victim flailing as she tries to steady herself on a landscape that has been drastically altered only for her. Her inevitable wipeout is then carefully documented by the Dragon as evidence of her lack of preparation, clear incompetence, and general unreliability, all which dictate the need to push her out.

> When my manager asked me for my login, while I was mid payroll, she changed the settings, then she completed two employees' payroll in the early hours of the morning, claiming I hadn't done it, when I was about to do it when I got in at 8 a.m. —*Office Worker*

> Teachers stole items from my classroom and home, and students were enlisted to do the same. Sleeping pills were put in my drink, it is sad how evil these people are. Damage was done to my car and home.

My keys were stolen in order for them to do this. Private investigators were hired to harass, stalk, defame and steal from me in order to cover-up the crimes and corruption and to prevent a lawsuit. —*Teacher*

The stock I needed to keep reordering was removed, relabeled, and I was accused of not doing my job properly. Also, the stationary I ordered from my budget for my job was removed, taken and when the person was asked if she had it, she started yelling at me. She was part of another manager's department and budget. I got into trouble for yelling back. I was so frustrated as this stuff happened over four months, and no one was listening to me. —*Administrator and Tutor*

My desk and computer were frequently tampered with, which included shocking graphic pornographic downloads that were never investigated, although I complained. I later brought it to the attention of the Board of Directors and filed a hostile work environment claim. I was interviewed by two of their attorneys. Although they had evidence and testimony, all of them took no action to hold anyone accountable. My female coworker, angry and upset, later screamed at me while speaking with the attorneys. I resigned. —*Fitness Professional*

#6—Gaslighting

The term gaslighting—manipulation of another by presenting an edited reality as fact—was derived from Patrick Hamilton's 1938 play titled *Gas Light*, which was later adopted for the screen. It documents the marital turmoil of Paul and Bella Mallen, in which Paul manipulates his wife into believing she is losing her grasp on reality, by moving objects and then claiming no participation, instead blaming her dwindling perceptual skills. Later, per the play's name, Paul lights the gaslight on the upper floor of their building to search for the riches the previous owner left behind after her murder. The lighting of these lamps, however, causes the lights below to flicker. When Bella comments on these fluctuations, she is made to believe it is her tie to reality, not the lights themselves, that is changing, making her think that she is experiencing the early stages of a psychological break. Later, it is revealed that her husband is not the upstanding citizen she thought she married but, instead, an adulterer, murderer, and bigamist set on orchestrating her demise.[4]

Like the movie, in workplace bullying, gaslighting is a conscious attempt by another to make the Creative believe that she misheard a conversation, read wrong a situation, or misinterpreted an event—a story line that makes the Creative question her perception of reality. Over time, as the Creative's view of the world is denied, her self-worth diminishes, making her doubt her experiences and competence at work, which eventually negatively impacts her job performance, resulting in a weakened state that makes her easier to control and manipulate.[5]

The Dragon is the master gaslighter, making the Creative believe that she didn't hear what she heard, see what she saw, or understand what she understood. The tsunami of mixed messages scrambles the Creative's worldview, making her question everything—most significantly, her own value and worth.

> The head of the department used those lies to discredit me, claiming I was unfit to perform my job. Gaslighting was his favorite method of undermining me, leading to neurotic behavior, thinking I was useless, and dangerous even to patients. He encouraged colleagues to steer clear of me, search for mistakes, keep a close eye on me, tell him anything I did, whether right or wrong. —*Psychologist*

> I have had the experience of having been given warning letter(s) over a three-year period, despite my quality performance, because my superiors gaslighted me and spread gossip throughout teams by exclusion and sabotage. —*Human Resources Employee*

#7—Ostracization

To exclude another is to push him out of the stadium, relegating him to a dark room to watch the events unfold on the screen instead of participating in the live experience. Ostracization, on the other hand, takes the impermanence of exclusion up a notch, permanently banishing the Creative from the community.[6] To be permanently othered from an organization in which you were once a valued contributing member is a gut-wrenching assault on one's personhood. As humans are naturally social animals, the act of ostracization leads to deep mortal wounds, resulting in significant health consequences, and at times, suicide.[7]

> I went from a beloved administrator with top evaluations to a complete outcast. Colleagues I ate lunch with each day and spent time with on weekends would no longer return my calls, texts, or emails. When I would pass them in the hall, they would pretend I was invisible. Though I was hurt by the bully, the treatment from people who I

thought were close friends is really what caused the deep wounding. I was so deeply traumatized I ended up quitting. To this day, I have never heard word one from people I once considered dear friends and confidants. —*School Principal*

#8—Retaliation

Creatives have an inner compass directing them to the right and righteousness, an innate calling to uphold the truth and diligently care for those they are charged to serve, whether they are children, students, patients, or clients. This internal calibration to tell the truth and speak up against injustices is dangerous, sure to ignite significant repercussions, including character assassination, mobbing, and eventual job loss.

The reverberations won't stop if and when the Creative is pushed out of the professional nest, for the Dragon's appetite for revenge will not be satiated until the Creative's reputation is crumpled and tattered, rendering her a throwaway and complete unknown.

I filed an EEO complaint and was blacklisted ever since. I also organized a project from scratch including a strategy that proved highly successful. It got high level recognition. Then it was taken from me, I was informed I mismanaged it. I was gaslighted and further work was taken away from me. I've been forced to look for another job elsewhere. —*U.S. Diplomat Aid Worker*

I was at a university and employed as a lecturer. I questioned some behavior of a fellow lecturer, which was blatantly discriminatory towards some students. I then became a victim of bullying—the discrimination was never addressed. I was forced to leave after taking legal support. —*Lecturer*

MORE WEAPONS OF CHOICE

Though the top eight tools of torture shared above were the tactics that emerged as the most salient themes in my research study, the following fifteen attack strategies scored a close second.

#9—Discriminate

The Dragon's monolithic view of the world requires her to keep her reports in straight lines and engaged in preapproved speech regarding topics rendered acceptable. Inside her whitewashed walls, the Dragon insists on uniformity, casting aside all strands of difference that may offer an alternative lens to her concocted reality defined as truth.

According to the Dragon, variations from her self-defined norms must be covered, erased, straightened, or disposed of whether such differences present as appearance, gender, sexuality, race, or age. Any veering from the center line results in the Creative being tossed in a file marked "For Immediate Disposal."

Appearance

I worked in finance for a large corporation. It was definitely controlled by men, and women were not encouraged to be promoted, especially if we had nice looks and smarts. —*Employee at a Large Corporation*

Gender

There are many instances in my four years under a bully principal. A good example would be that my principal, who seemed to have an issue with men, hired a qualified instructor to direct my jazz ensemble without my involvement and also took pep rally playing opportunities from my band to demonstrate that a man may not always be in charge. —*Band Director*

Sexuality

I was bullied by my supervisor because she had issues with my sexuality and my choice of partners . . . I was bullied, intimidated, belittled and humiliated in a work-related training run by a psychologist. After I complained about the training, the council I worked for bullied me harder. I ended up complaining about all past harassment and discrimination I had endured in my ten years of service, and they crucified me. —*Records Manager*

Race

> It has been nearly thirty years since I worked for someone who I was
> absolutely convinced had my back and encouraged me to be creative
> and supported me taking reasonable risks. That was also the last time
> that I was directly supervised by another person of color. —*Fire and
> Emergency Services*

Age

> I needed to decide if I wanted to return to that school building or try
> to transfer out to a different building. I decided that I didn't want to
> return and retired at age sixty-two. The bottom line was . . . anyone
> over fifty in that building and in that organization is not respected. I
> was made to feel like I was incompetent and couldn't do my job. —
> *Teacher's Aide*

#10—Hurt Students, Patients, or Clients to Frame the Creative

It seems unconscionable: a headmistress putting the welfare of children at risk to shut down an administrator's big thinking; a floor
nurse altering a patient's file, with potentially deadly repercussions,
in a ploy to paint an RN as incompetent; or a financial analyst, trad-
ing without permission, a client's portfolio in order to orchestrate a
mistake that would wrongly cost a Creative his job. However, such
reports weave through the narratives of the brave Creatives who
boldly told their story of how their destruction played out through
the fate of another, innocent bystanders unaware of their placement
as pawns in a game they didn't know they were playing.

> They would rarely return my calls, emails and lose my documents.
> They would even be rude to my customers to spite me. It got so bad
> one customer threatened to leave her quarter million dollar account
> if I didn't come back (I was on military leave). —*Financial Services
> Employee*

#11—Enlist Flying Monkeys

Think back to *The Wizard of Oz*, when the winged monkeys in
Baum's tale shared with Dorothy a warning of what's to come if she
continues walking down the yellow brick road with aspirations of
something greater.[8]

Flying monkeys, however, do not just hover in fantastical stories, but dart and dive down the halls of schools, universities, hospitals, companies, and nonprofits armed with sharp antennas, gathering intel and dropping cryptic messages from the Dragon onto the victim's path to unsettle the calm.

Flying monkeys enable the Dragon to extend her claws through the reach of another, downloading messages, asserting control, and creating the disquieting commotion of always being watched. Sometimes flying monkeys can be innocent bystanders, such as the Community Builders introduced earlier, unaware that they are being manipulated into participating in the denigration of another, under the guise of goodwill.[9]

> She relies on her direct assistant to be her eyes and ears. In time, the bullying was directed at me in subtle ways, I was singled out from others for being late, ideas and suggestions were dismissed (or maybe that were represented as the direct assistant's ideas and I never knew), and I had to jump through hoops to get a company cell phone even after a year of employment while others got theirs as part of their new hire package once their ninety day trial period ended. —*Administrator in a Nonprofit*

#12—"Interview" Colleagues to Get Dirt

"Do you have time to talk?" the conversation may go, as the Creative's boss or colleague engages a coworker in an off-the-record, informal interview predicated on spreading a curated narrative in which the Dragon's victim is labeled a troublemaker and an under-the-hat warning is issued that the interviewee may want to start excluding the victim or risk "becoming part of the problem."

Following the initial download, leading questions are often dropped, most asked by someone with more power to someone with less power, with direct undertones of the types of answers that will protect the interviewee from becoming targeted next. It may sound something like this: "So, Travon, lots of people are complaining that Tricia isn't able to deliver to the team. Can you tell me of a time when Tricia dropped the ball?" Or, "Laura—we have been getting lots of reports that Tricia has been rude to her colleagues. It would be a great help to me and Tricia if you could share a time when you found her to be rude? After all, I only want to help Tricia be the best version of herself."

These informal leading interviews, most likely conducted by the Dragon or one of her Shapeshifters, will then be relayed as fact to Human Resources and typed up as gospel.

Suddenly, these off-the-record conversations become on-the-record personnel files that read, "We are concerned about Tricia. Earlier this week, one of her colleagues expressed his concern that she was not able to fulfill her job responsibilities, and several others shared specific incidents in which she was rude or demanding to another colleague."

Of course, when Tricia inquires about who said these things and under what circumstances, the retort will simply be, "We have an abundance of colleagues expressing their concern regarding your work ethic, follow-through, and professional demeanor." At this point, the ball of Tricia's career is starting to pick up speed as it careens down the hill of her future, fueled by lies, innuendos, and intimidations. Regardless, she will not be allowed a rebuttal or granted an investigation into the process, for the lies have been turned to truth.

They started asking employees behind my back in "secret" if they felt bullied by me. So employees started telling me about the witch hunt. I consulted with a union lead . . . which resulted in him creating a text group with them naming me and laughing, forming secret meetings, and talking about me. Employees also showed me this.
—*Nurse*

My superintendent started informally interviewing the teachers who reported to me. She would drop into their classroom under the guise of being interested in their work and wanting to connect with students, but as soon as they were alone in the room, she would pose leading questions like, "I have a number of people who say Fran is a bad principal and that parents and students are complaining. I know you are an excellent teacher, and I want to make sure you don't get swept up in the controversy once we bring these concerns forward. I imagine some people may lose their jobs, and I want to protect you of course. Could you please share your opinion and experience of Fran?"
—*School Principal*

#13—Take Advantage of Poor Health

Creatives often self-identify as empathizers, deeply feeling and thoughtfully aware of small changes in themselves, other people, and the environment. At times, they breathe in, full force, the all-encompassing pain of colleagues; in those moments, they stand vigilant, offering their compassion and support. This behavioral disposition leaves the Creative flabbergasted and unprepared when the Dragon takes advantage of a time when the Creative is enduring great emotional or physical suffering.

The Dragon, too, picks up on others' silent, private turmoil, but instead of wrapping it in a care package and gently asking, "How are you?" she stores it in her arsenal to be discharged as a weapon at the first moment of vulnerability. She is a master at finding the Creative's exposed skin, holding it over the fire, and then acting surprised as he burns.

> At the time, I was in clinical treatment for depression and anxiety and the supervisor was aware of this. He targeted me with threats that escalated my mental illness until I suffered a breakdown in my workplace. I had to be taken to the local hospital for sedation and was unable to return to work for months. —*Technology Consultant*

> I have alopecia and psoriasis. After I questioned a supervisory note, in a concerned, not insubordinate way, my three supervisors started micromanaging my work and would send me emails "needing to talk." They made comments about my appearance. It caused me to have a bout of bulimia, which I had conquered years before. I've since transferred to another location where I feel safe and appreciated. — *Mental Health Worker*

> Ever since I returned to work after cancer treatment, the staff member who was covering my teaching commitment, resented my return and was negative about everything I did. —*Head of School*

#14—Disclose Personal Medical Information

Employees are people with families, health hiccups, and challenges. Though they attempt to put them aside when they come to work, they can sometimes have a negative effect. In an effort to lessen the blow, some Creatives feel called to share in confidence with their boss that they are navigating debilitating migraines, starting chemotherapy, seeking support for their depression, or dealing with the unpredictable flare-ups of lupus. These conversations are meant as a small window into their private struggles to explain why at times they may need to step out early, take a longer lunch break, or appear not quite their typical joyful selves. In return for their honest disclosure, they expect that information to be held in confidence. Unfortunately, the Dragon grabs these explanations and uses them as weapons against the Creative when she is tragically at her most vulnerable.

> My boss disclosed my medical condition to another staff member and told her that I exaggerate the condition for sympathy, despite me having not mentioned it to any staff members, and it being serious enough for me to need surgery every six months in a two year period. —*Teacher*

#15—Withhold Advancement Opportunities

The Dragon exudes control, a stark reminder that the Creative is simply a puppet in her play titled *Psychological Terrorism at Work*. The Dragon finds it imperative that the Creative stays small, keeping her wings clipped. To keep the puppet strings taut, when others recognize the Creative's dynamism, deep content reservoirs, and innovative spirit, and hence offers her a ladder to the next level, the Dragon will swiftly kick it out from under her feet, leaving her crashing to the ground, wounded, unable to get back up and try again. Any opportunity offered to the Creative is seen as a direct threat to the Dragon's reign, and thus she discredits, silences, and openly sabotages all upward mobility, assuring that the Creative stays in her windowless room, unable to see a brighter future.

> I have tried to move several times to a new Department where I would be a better fit. However, my Dean will drop innuendos about me to ruin my chances. I can't get another job because she roadblocks all opportunities. —*Professor*

#16—Give Falsified Reviews

Most teachers, professors, nurses, doctors, analysts, lawyers, and managers are subjected to yearly or biyearly reviews documenting their performance and providing feedback for growth opportunities. Often, such reviews are tied to compensation and promotion possibilities and live in perpetuity in personnel files.

Before a Creative encounters a Dragon, his reviews are typically off-the-chart excellent, glowing, all arrows pointing to the box marked "top performer." These commendations may stack up over decades, punctuated with awards hanging on his office wall. Then, suddenly, without warning or provocation, a grenade is launched, and the Creative is described as subpar.

As the attacks intensify, the Creative watches as a brand-new narrative is written, in which his superstar status has been downgraded to a deviant and a letdown. It may seem outlandish to think that schools, hospitals, and companies would falsify reports to sabotage another and impede his upward trajectory; unfortunately, as you will hear from the voices of Creatives, it is a common theme that emerged from my case studies. Often, the initial fabrication in the denigrating report is the Creative's first sign that he has become the Dragon's prey.

I had been a top performer yet was given a scathing review by a manager who I never reported to. —*Sales Executive*

Once my old manager retired things started getting really bad. I was being targeted, set up, belittled, and so on. I was written up for the first time in twenty-seven years. Due to the report, I had work I had always done taken away from me. I was also removed from committees. She would not talk to me directly. Several months later, I was written up again by her, stating that others complained about my behavior. I was very upset. I knew that something was going on. I was told by her that it was my tone. She told me to reel it in. —*Nurse*

When we had a perfect state inspection, she fired me. The reason was I took a long lunch one day. However, that was a lie. I wasn't even in the building. I was in a different county at a conference. —*Nurse*

#17—Micromanage

Creatives, by nature, are independent global thinkers, tinkerers who fit and fiddle as they work toward finding solutions for problems the organization hasn't even identified. On top of their big-hat thinking, Creatives are experts in their field, exhibiting deep knowledge that often far surpasses their superiors.

Therefore, when a Dragon wants to sharpen her claws, she will attempt to make the Creative's room quite small, covering the window where the ideas flood in, insisting on regular, extended meetings in which the Dragon details directions to projects that surpass her level of sophistication. All of this micromanaging weighs heavily on the Creative's motivation, often prompting her to look for the exit after realizing that the ceilings in her current job are too low for her to soar.

> It started with new excessive control and micro-management and impossible and unreasonable demands. —*College Lecturer*

#18—Prohibit Collaborations

The Dragon's power comes from controlling people, conversations, and circumstances. When ideas across programs and departments collide, and world experiences join in a common cause, the energy created is empowering and intoxicating. When people start to talk, mosaicking together their diverse lenses, colors of imagination explode, and beautiful things are painted. This type of innovation, however, is collective and vast, way too wide open for the Dragon to control. Therefore, she insists on a strict hierarchy, where people stay seated and never whisper to the person sitting in front of them. To the Dragon, a quiet, controlled office is a fine place to be.

> My boss would change her mind about what she wanted and would tell me I could not speak with people in other departments about the work they needed me to do, which made it pretty much impossible for me to do my work, or she would rewrite my work multiple times. —*Communications Director*

> Those first three years I blindly did everything I could to make the job work, constantly having to prove I hadn't made mistakes, constantly trying to find ways to correct historical mistakes which weren't of my making, spending twice as long doing everything as I tried to find work-arounds for the badly set up software and systems I kept being told were as they should be. My boss continued to question everything I did and constantly put me down, not allowing me to collaborate with others. —*Finance Manager*

#19—Take Away Responsibilities

The Creative has great loves that draw him into work each morning, singing a song of possibilities. The Creative's love may be writing, directing, manufacturing, or building collaborations that make the school, university, hospital, company, or nonprofit stronger.

It doesn't take long to find out what makes the Creative's heart beat with anticipation, but that is the very thing the Dragon identifies and then rips away. By design, the Dragon steals the one thing that matters most to the Creative through accusation of incompetence, hence not only robbing the Creative of her motivation but stepping on her self-worth for all to witness, a warning to others.

The professor who is an expert writer might be told by her dean that all grant emails must garner her approval before being sent out, for certainly the professor's wordcrafting can't be trusted. Or perhaps the doctor, who has led three successful recent studies in her lab, is told her funding is on hold until her recent results can be verified by a colleague who the Creative knows lacks the necessary expertise to judge its validity.

All of these "taking aways" are done only to shrink the Creative's spirit, reach, and success, over time causing her to doubt that she ever had the talent, capability, and wherewithal to perform at her past near perfection.

> Over three to four years she took work away work I had been doing for well over a decade and gave it to the other two. She then canceled some of my projects and gave me lots of grief about my work schedule and start time, so that I began to work unpaid overtime nearly every day and my self-confidence was shot. —*Communications Director*

#20—Make False Accusations

The Dragon often comes up empty on ideas, so she learns to make it easy on herself by demanding little creativity when it comes to building her mythical world. Instead, she becomes a boomerang, lobbing accusations that come her way right back at the accuser. Due to the often-present power imbalance, her violent returns stick.

For example, when a Dragon is accused of stealing, she paints the accuser as a thief. When the Dragon is told she is rude, she calls her finger-pointer belligerent. And when the Dragon is identified as a troublemaker, she takes the label off her jacket and places it squarely on the back of her competition.

Whatever label is placed upon her, she returns with vigor, passionately calling out the accuser as guilty. Unfortunately, the strategy often works, for in cultures that lack transparency, where toxic interactions are used as tools of war, an accusation can become truth in the blink of an eye, no verification or evidence required.

Reporting it to the managers at the very top did nothing. I was made out to be a troublemaker. —*Recreation Therapist*

One day a woman in another team lodged a formal complaint that I had bullied her. I was devastated, but also confused. I didn't even work with this woman. Apparently her complaint rested on some information provided by another colleague. The organization accepted the complaint, sent me home and brought in an independent investigator. A few weeks later another complaint was lodged against me by a new graduate in my team, who was open that she had help writing it. The organization decided to treat this complaint formally too. A group of staff then lodged a series of official information requests to have my emails released. The organization released my email correspondence to them (which included emails requesting support from my manager and HR), which they used to add further details to their complaints. They complained that by speaking to my manager and HR I was attempting to destroy their reputations. The organization then decided to launch a third investigation into me. —*Manager at a Government Agency*

I was accused of theft and I was hounded and bullied and persecuted. —*Social Worker*

My boss filed a fabricated complaint of sexual misconduct against me, and the agency I work for has continuously refused to help me or the other victims of management's targeting and harassment. —*Immigration Officer*

#21—Move Offices

Through an old but effective strategy, if you can't remove an employee from her job, move her office to a place that will make her want to quit. It sounds outlandish at first blush: put a tenured chemistry professor in the basement of the social work building, move a financial analyst to the attic that lacks Wi-Fi to access necessary databases, or require a fitness instructor to teach and train in a room with no mirrors or air conditioning. Unfortunately, it is a common but effective tactic Dragons use to denigrate others in the hope that they will pack their bags and leave, avoiding the paperwork necessary to terminate a top performer.

> They moved my office, I suspect to get me to quit. —*Health-Care Worker*

> He began to keep information from me, didn't invite me into meetings I had been in previously, he pulled resources that I'd been given to do my job, and he falsified information about me on three years of job evaluations. He also expected me to work in below freezing temperatures, even though I was ill and was on FMLA for a respiratory problem caused by his putting me into an office with a mold issue. —*Education Outreach Administrator*

#22—Make the Creative Too Sick to Work

The Dragon plots how to get the Creative to step off her game, directing the spotlight back to the Dragon breathing fire and eliminating the Creative from competition. Murder and maiming are off the table, so the Dragon uses manipulation, sabotage, gaslighting, and exclusion, as well as the other crafty tactics previously mentioned to slowly break the Creative's health, driving her into emotional and physical debilitation, unable to work. This loss of the Creative's work identity further drives her into perpetual darkness, struggling to find herself.

> When I read about mobbing, it becomes clear how and why I was targeted, but that is cold comfort. I am not working, but I am in therapy, trying to find my way back to myself. I felt deeply traumatized and damaged by the experience, and I am afraid I won't be able to cope if I ever return to a leadership position or any job. —*Patient Education Director*

As an able-bodied individual in my mid thirties, I have now been unemployed for the last three and a half years (functionally disabled from workplace related PTSD), with my husband having to become my de facto caregiver, assisting me with most activities of daily living. —*Physician*

#23—Prevent Creative from Getting a New Job

A Dragon's revenge is piercing, running deep below the waters of reciprocity and fair play. When a Dragon sets her claw on the Creative, she will not remove her nails until the destruction is complete. In other words, belittlement is just the prelude, character dismemberment is the first act, and job loss makes for an appealing intermission. Not until the Creative's physical and emotional health explode and her future job prospects are deemed a wistful fantasy will the play conclude and outward destruction cease. It is the Creative's inner obliteration that she must repair to be herself again.

In this way, the Dragon is a virus that gets inside the Creative and infects every kernel of her being even after she relinquishes her name badge and access card in hopes of a more peaceful future.

One Saturday, I received a special delivery letter from the university president ordering me to undergo a complete psychiatric assessment with a specific doctor at a specific hospital. There was no way to be "normal" with a conventional male psychiatrist. Besides, I was very upset from months of bullying. I did not know about the Americans with Disability Act, which I could have used to gain equality in the department. So, I packed up my office and house and left the state. Later, when I interviewed for academic positions and the prospective employer would call my old job for a reference, the message was, "We have a legal agreement not to say anything." I had been the number one candidate for 2 positions until that phone call. I gave up searching for a job in my academic specialty. These 2 men destroyed my life. My specialty was my life. They took it. —*Professor*

Yes, I am destroyed professionally. —*Civil Engineer*

CONCLUSION

Dragons are a noxious lot, forced to avoid tactics that leave physical marks, thus relegating them to weaponizing words, withholding resources, and rewriting plotlines to scripts of desperation and despair. The Dragon wields her weapons masterfully, squelching the Creative's motivation, forcing him to look away from the sun, as she moves his office to the cellar, hoping he will fade into the darkness. At first encounter, the Dragon's toolbox overflows with mysterious ammunition, but once the Creative shines the spotlight, revealing her strategies, he gains the superpower of anticipation, readying himself to defend his perimeter, allowing his light to keep shining.

INVITATION #5

Envision your Dragon sitting at her desk, fire shooting up on either side of her throne. To the right, is a large toolbox filled with all of the weapons she used in her quest to denigrate your character. Now, fold a page of your journal in half the long way. Label the first column "Tools" and the second column "Examples." Record each tool she has wielded against you with accompanying examples. Now look at your list. Were there certain tools she relied on more heavily than others? Did her tools become more underhanded and damaging as the war progressed? Are there tools she used that are not mentioned in this chapter? Does identifying the Dragon's tactics help you to better understand your bullying story? If you are still in the mud of the war, does naming her tools help you to anticipate what might happen next? What tools do you use to maintain your health and integrity?

Chapter 5

This Job Is Making Me Sick

LOSING MYSELF

I can't quite remember when I was whole. When I could run my hands across my body and feel every part of me.

INTRODUCTION

Victims of workplace abuse are often given neatly wrapped packages of well-meaning yet misinformed advice such as "just ignore them" or "don't take what happens at work so seriously."

These sentiments, though perhaps apropos when negotiating rude service at the grocery store, miss the mark when it comes to dealing with psychological terrorism on the job. Further, such remarks unintentionally dismiss and devalue the trauma of workplace abuse and its resulting long-term and significant health consequences.

So, why is workplace bullying so devastating and, at times, deadly to its victims?

Though a variety of theories have been floated over the past decade, Erving Goffman's theory of stigma and Harold Garfinkel's conception of the degradation ceremony best capture for me the destruction, though neither were applying their theories to workplace abuse.[1]

Below, I will make that connection. But first, I want you to hear from a finance executive, in her own words, whose world was unexpectedly shattered with calamitous results.

I spent the first three years totally confused as to what was happening to me, mainly blaming myself and unwittingly feeding my bully with more information than they could have hoped for as I shared my woes with them about how uncomfortable my job was despite endless hours of effort and people-pleasing. I had never found myself in a position like this before. I was hardworking, not put off by a challenge, friendly, and experienced. I got on with people. I'm really easy to work with. I was baffled and slowly broken. Then I spent three years trying to excuse, fix, understand and cope with the bullying. Then another two years blocking out the bullying, pushing myself to the limits, and ultimately planning my exit. But it didn't come soon enough, and eventually, I was mobbed into a black hole of despair. I left broken, angry and silenced. —*Finance Executive*

So, what might have happened here to this well-liked, hard-working employee who was an expert in her field and had amassed a long history of professional success? The answer, unbeknownst to her at the time: she was stigmatized and subjected to a public shunning, also known as a degradation ceremony.

WHAT DOES IT MEAN TO BE STIGMATIZED?

To be stigmatized is to be othered, cast out of the community, and branded an untouchable. Animals do it in the wild, and Dragons do it in the workplace. The result of both, however, is the same. The victim, who has been put outside the walls that protect the herd, is left alone and vulnerable, with no resources to defend herself against the environment, eventually leading to her real or metaphorical demise.

According to Goffman, a preeminent Canadian American sociologist, a stigma is a marker placed upon an individual, due to her difference, which labels her as pestilent, thus relegating her to the bottom rung of the societal hierarchy, a public shunning that ensures her demise.[2]

Why are victims of workplace bullying stigmatized? According to my research, Creatives fall prey to psychological terrorism on the job for one or more of three reasons:

1. First, the Creative is unique in some way. Outwardly or inwardly, she presents differently per her thinking, philosophy,

race, gender, sexual orientation, religious beliefs, neurodiversity, or some other characteristic.
2. Second, she is an innovator. She pushes the boundaries of tradition, which recalibrates the status quo, hence shaking the Dragon's established hierarchy.
3. Third, she is a whistle-blower. She calls out bad, unethical, and at times illegal behavior in order to protect the students, patients, clients, or community members she is charged to serve.

This is ironic, for outside the nonsensical world of workplace abuse, all of these characteristics strengthen an institution's performance, productivity, and contributions to their community.

Unfortunately, in bullying cultures, once stigmatized, the degradation ceremony will commence, and there is rarely an effective vaccine to stop the progression and fallout.

THE DEGRADATION CEREMONY

A degradation ceremony, as it applies to workplace bullying, is a public shunning that systematically hijacks a Creative's work story and rebrands her as a danger to the social structure and productivity of an organization, thus attempting to justify the unspeakable acts of the participants.

As an avid reader and researcher, over the past four years I have been on a concerted search for an explanation of workplace bullying that encapsulates the inhumane and, at times, deadly repercussions of workplace abuse. For bullying on the job is not a personality conflict or a professional disagreement—but the purposeful dismantling of a person's character, stripping her of her accomplishments and fortitude, as a strategy for convincing and enlisting others to join in on her ceremonial and permanent excommunication from the community.

What Is a Degradation Ceremony?

In 1956, Harold Garfinkel, a preeminent sociologist and ethnomethodologist at the University of California in Los Angeles, published a paper titled *Conditions of a Successful Degradation Ceremony* in which he defined a degradation ceremony as "any communicative work between persons, whereby the public identity of an actor is transformed into something looked on as lower in the local scheme of social types."[3] Though Garfinkel did not reference workplace bullying in his research, from my own personal experiences and the stories of more than two hundred brave Creatives who shared their narratives with me, it is the first explanation that accurately encapsulates the devastation of workplace abuse and explains the tragic, long-term health consequences of being subjected to psychological terrorism on the job.

How Does a Degradation Ceremony Unfold?

The degradation ceremony is initiated and carried out by the Dragon. In this role, her voice is omnipotent and beyond rebuke. She writes the rule book and redefines reality according to her evolving script. As discussed in chapter 2, the Dragon is draconian, her power dependent on the unmitigated control of the Shapeshifters and the silence of the Community Builders.

A precipitating event serves as the degradation ceremony's prelude, in which the Creative breaks institutional norms by presenting differently, thinking innovatively, or calling out bad, unethical, or illegal behavior. This may look like a professor who talks openly about her same-sex partner; a nurse who proposes a new mentoring program, backed by research, that varies significantly from the outdated approach the hospital has used over the past decade; or perhaps an accountant who points out a discrepancy in the branch's budget over the previous fiscal year.

Such actions prompt the Dragon to evaluate whether the Creative has gone "beyond the pale," a phrase meaning stake, derived from the Latin word *palus*. This idea first entered our lexicon amid the fourteenth century Norman invasion in which imposing stakes were strategically placed around the king's territory, a foreboding blockade to deter attack.

Today, the phrase is used to signify when an individual questions, challenges, or steps outside the cultural norms of a family or organization, unsettling the power structure and prompting the community to expel her from the protective fold of the institution, leaving her vulnerable and alone.[4]

In the workplace, if a Dragon deduces that an individual has breached the perimeter, or gone beyond the pale, the Dragon will ring the bell, alerting Shapeshifters and Community Builders that the ceremony is about to commence.

Because the Creative has social power, is thought of as kind and compassionate, and possesses an extensive history of success and innovation, the degradation ceremony's eventual expulsion cannot be based on performance or seen as a personal and unprovoked attack. Instead, a much more dubious and sinister strategy must be employed, one that obliterates the Creative's persona through character assassination in which she is portrayed as a dangerous impostor who poses an immediate threat to the organization's stability and success.

The degradation ceremony begins with the Dragon firing a warning shot to voice her displeasure in the form of gossip and exclusion to bring the Creative back into compliance with organizational expectations. Institutions that use degradation ceremonies as tools of control tend to subscribe to cultural norms that demand loyalty, enforce hierarchies, discourage curiosity, value appearance, and tolerate or encourage unethical behavior.

Following the warning shot, if the Creative continues to authentically inhabit her difference, embrace her innovative spirit, or call out the organization's bad behavior, the degradation ceremony switches its goal from enforced compliance to character assassination, in which the Creative is systematically and permanently "othered."

To entice colleagues and leadership to participate in the othering process, the denouncer asserts righteous indignation over the Creative's actions, declaring her deeds indicative of an innately flawed character that poses an existential threat to the organization's future and asserting that the only way to prevent calamity is the Creative's immediate exile. This, of course, is ironic, because the Creative is likely a highly ethical, caring, and innovative visionary, the very type of person the organization requires to evolve positively.

Unfortunately, this carefully crafted approach creates a dynamic in which colleagues must align with the Dragon to maintain their "good person status" or risk being seen as part of the problem and thus targeted next. As a result, most colleagues will join ranks with the Dragon, standing in solidarity against the person who just yesterday they looked up to and called friend.

To complete the "othering" process, the Dragon hijacks the Creative's narrative, flips her script, and engages in a full rewrite of the past. The first step in this reality revision is to establish that the Creative's past accomplishments and accolades either didn't happen or were wrongly bestowed. The second step is to plant rapid-growth seeds of gossip that entangle her being, cover up her good nature, and portray an alternate and false identity. To accomplish this task, the Dragon will often accuse the Creative of the very same behavior that the Dragon engages in daily, such as stealing, manipulating, or participating in unethical or illegal behavior.

This second step is particularly essential in gaining the support of Community Builders, for they must have stories to grab onto in order to justify their decision to turn on the very person who supported them during hardships, bolstered their career, and sat with them over countless lunches swapping family stories.

The third and final step of the degradation ceremony requires the Dragon to activate people's fear, convincing them the organization's success and their careers will be in peril if the Creative is not immediately excommunicated from the institution. At this point in the ceremony, the unmitigated attacks cause the Creative heart palpitations, high blood pressure, and migraine attacks, to name just a few significant health consequences. In tandem with the physical decline, anxiety and depression settle in, impeding her daily functioning. The loss of her identity, friendships, and professional life shame her, leaving her with long-term confusion and grief.

The degradation ceremony concludes once the Creative is cast out, gutted and unrecognizable to herself as her former colleagues go out for drinks to celebrate her demise, denying personal responsibility for the slaying by exchanging sentiments of "for the good of the company, it simply had to be done."

PHYSICAL AND EMOTIONAL CONSEQUENCES OF WORKPLACE BULLYING

The degradation ceremony, thus initiated by the Dragon and supported by the organization, transforms a once healthy and successful Creative into a shell of her former self, leaving her body aching, her heart hurting, and her career in shards outside her now locked office door.[5]

The ceremony shatters the Creative's belief in a benevolent world, where people are ethical and organizations do the right things for those they are charged to serve, leaving no remnants of her former reality, where people are good, and institutions can be trusted.[6]

Though workplace bullying leads to a significant decline in the Creative's physical health and emotional well-being, the division between the two is nebulous, the resulting damage equally devastating, as desribed by the Creative below.

> When I returned to work, my boss behaved shockingly towards me. Other staff confided in me some of the terrible things shared when I was out. I was so devastated by the gossip that it started to impact me physically, resulting in two unexplained losses of consciousness, which after extensive testing, the Neurologist contributed to extreme stress. As a result, I lost my driver's license, and despite requesting confidentiality, my boss found not so subtle ways to let people know I could no longer drive into meetings. —*Local Community Director*

Most of the symptoms detailed below, when they originated, were mild and only occurred directly following one of the Dragon's attacks. Over time, however, the conditions worsened, as the Creative anticipated the likelihood of another confrontation. Eventually, the pain was present and all encompassing, constantly activated, regardless of whether the Creative was at work, at home, or on vacation as expressed by this Creative.

> I'm still trying to get over the emotional terror of this job. It is always with me. —*Recreational Therapist*

Below I share the seventeen health complications that emerged consistently across my data and are supported by the research of others. Intermixed with each explanation are firsthand accounts of Creative's experiences. Inside these stories, Creatives mention several complications within a single sharing, for workplace bullying equates to a full-body attack with conflating health repercussions. Some of the health consequences listed below are medical diagnoses such as heart attacks or depression, others are behaviors such as absenteeism, and a few are forced actions such as medical leave.

#1—Intense Feelings of Injustice

When I read Creatives' accounts of the abuse they suffered and speak to them for several hours over Zoom, most express a deep need for justice, yearning for those who detonated a bomb in the middle of their career to be held accountable for the damages done.[7]

> It is amazing the human capacity for having multiple situations occur at the same time while maintaining the capacity for joy, gratitude, and the simple enjoyment of life. These criminal acts committed against me that resulted in constant dark clouds looming over my head, are always here with me. To cast them away, I need justice. I need them to get what they deserve. —*Caregiver*

#2—Trouble Sleeping

Humans require adequate sleep to maintain their physical bodies and emotional stability. Sleep gives the Creative a chance to recharge and reestablish a sense of equilibrium. However, the trauma of workplace abuse wages an ongoing war on the Creative, creating a continual internal dialogue that makes it virtually impossible to drift into slumber. This lack of rest disrupts the Creative's level of homeostasis, making him more vulnerable to anxiety and depression.[8]

> I didn't quite realize it at the time, but the health decline that I suffered was a direct result of all of the stress. I lost about a third of my hair, suffered insomnia, gained fifty pounds, without any change in my personal habits, which would not respond to diet or exercise, and developed skin problems. It's been one year since the abuse stopped and I'm just now beginning to see some physical healing. —*Human Services Manager*

> I was frightened, broken, regularly suffering panic attacks, and unable to sleep or eat. My reputation was in tatters. The investigations had been so public, but the outcome was kept private. I was isolated, while the perpetrators remained in their jobs, free to talk and spread their lies. —*Government Worker*

#3—Weight Fluctuation

A Creative's weight is not simply a mathematical formula or statistic; sometimes it serves as a barometer of her experience in the world of work. Disruptions in her family life and on the job can make her weight move up or down the scale. This fluctuation is particularly difficult for women, who are often judged by their dress size instead of their résumé. When Creatives are bullied at work, they may react by restricting their eating, thus quite literally shrinking who they are, or overeat as a strategy for seeking comfort in a world suddenly so uncomfortable.[9]

> I was isolated, at home, unable to interact with anyone in the workplace and scared I was going crazy or I might lose my job. I had to start anti-anxiety medication, I lost a lot of weight and lost all ability to look after myself. —*Government Employee*

#4— Gastrointestinal Issues, Heart Palpitations, and Migraines

Often a Creative does not realize he is being bullied until he visits his primary care physician to seek help for a stomach issue, an irregular heartbeat, or debilitating migraines. As the physician gathers the Creative's medical history, she uncovers what appears to be a steady exposure to a toxic work culture. To garner a deeper understanding, throughout the visit she peppers the Creative with questions about his typical workday. Through that conversation, she slowly uncovers the link between his physical symptoms and the psychological attacks he is enduring at work.

> I've experienced physical decomposition from workplace abuse. Due to chest pain and insomnia, I had to seek medical care and go on medication. I have lost days to headaches and paranoia has consumed my days off. When I am able to gather my strength enough to go into work, I find I have lost my ability to focus. —*Nurse*

#5—Burnout

Physical pain and emotional turmoil can result in complete exhaustion, ultimately rendering the Creative unable to work. Over time, small seeds of burnout explode into major depression and other debilitating health consequences.[10]

As I was on ACC leave recovering, my immediate boss told people I banged my head and went psycho, that I was milking the injury and that I was mentally ill. —*Community Developer*

#6—Absenteeism and Presenteeism

Workplace bullying places the Creative amid a storm of chaos in which one minute she is praised for a job well done and the next is belittled in front of colleagues, publicly admonished for being incompetent. The instability of the workplace culture leaves the Creative in a constant state of unrest, resulting in an intense need to always be present, even when ill, a phenomenon referred to as "presenteeism," or charging her to leave the office, a similar but opposing phenomenon described as "absenteeism." Both phenomena grow out of what researchers describe as the conservation of resources theory, in which employees feel they must be present at work to keep their current position or must be absent to maintain and protect their health.[11]

> Each morning I arrived at work close to six in the morning, hoping that if I was always present in the building, I could prove my worth, help the children, and then the attacks would subside. Each time I left, I felt they were concocting a plan for my dismissal. Unfortunately, my intuition proved to be true. It turns out, the very person I was trying to help to secure a job was the same person who was conniving to get mine. It made me feel like I could never get away or take a break from the turmoil. Spending all of my waking hours in that building slowly murdered my spirit. The negativity and gaslighting were coercive. — *School Principal*

#7—A Decline in Confidence and Self-Worth

As shared in chapter 2, Creatives of workplace bullying are typically well-liked, top performers who are experts in their field. Prior to the abuse, they enjoy a strong sense of purpose and self-worth. Following a series of attacks, their confidence slowly ebbs, making it slippery to walk, causing them to be ever mindful of when they may fall next, fully believing that they are no longer worthy of being caught. Instead, they surrender to the suggestion to shrink down to the smallest version of themselves, quiet and afraid.[12]

I had gone from being a highly confident person within my profession to a total wreck. —*Manager*

#8—Feelings of Fear Prompting Withdrawal

As humans, Creatives are naturally social animals, even introverts like me. However, when a community turns divisive, and colleagues that the Creative once shared laughs with over lunch pass her in the hall without acknowledgment, she begins to question the safety of connection. To open up to another requires an expectation of reciprocity. When that social contract is broken, especially in relationships she considered strong, the world suddenly feels askew; places that once felt wild with possibilities now feel exclusionary and narrow. To protect herself, she withdraws, resulting in intense feelings of loneliness and alienation.[13]

> Even now, three years on, I still have trust issues. I often find it difficult to mix with my colleagues in my new post, even though they are lovely and sweet folks. I was once quite a bubbly sort of person, but now I prefer to be quiet and just sit in a corner, do my work to the best of my ability, because I'm always wondering if it may happen again. —*Senior Manager*

#9—Anxiety and Panic Attacks

The Dragon is quite a crafty creature, throwing her prey off his game by complimenting his performance after last week's pitch and offering an invitation for afternoon tea to celebrate, then following up the very next day with a volatile public rebuke at the company-wide meeting. Such behavior creates a Tilt-A-Whirl reality, inciting panic and anxiety about what may happen next.[14]

> Now I suffer from panic attacks, agoraphobia, and I have lost my job and two and a half years of my life. I am suicidal. —*Computer Analyst*

> Several years ago, I had a nervous breakdown after seven plus years of bullying at work. Two bosses and a co-worker initiated the abuse and maligned and humiliated me repeatedly and publicly, gaslighted me, and excluded me, holding back information and making it difficult for me to be effective. —*Development Officer*

#10—Shame

Victims of workplace bullying tend to be experts in their field with impressive performance records, often sought after for advice and counsel. When a Dragon places a target on their backs, the character assassination, belittlement, and tirades chip away at the Creative's confidence and joy, over time impacting his ability to maintain peak performance. This understandable decline brings about shame, as he no longer recognizes the person peering back at him in the mirror.[15]

> Now I am beside myself. I have already had to be seen by a doctor due to the anxiety that I was being subjected to, and for chest pain, high blood pressure and high heart rate. —*Nurse*

> Bullying and disruptive antisocial behaviors have no business in an office or school environment. They are caustic and damaging to office teams, negatively impacting creativity and productivity and are psychologically harmful. The inability to get my work done in an efficient manner greatly caused me stress and anxiety. I felt fearful and paranoid because of the hostility I experienced. —*Exercise Fitness Professional*

#11—Depression

Work is more than a building the Creative spends his hours in during the week; it is a community in which he seeks inspiration, support, and connection as he attempts to contribute to the greater good. In that community the Creative takes his place on a team and develops long-term friendships as he works toward common aspirations. However, when a Dragon severs the ties with his coworkers, withdraws the work that feeds his spirit, and tosses rumors into the office gossip mill, the space that once served as a source of comfort becomes a capsule of despair. As the Creative feels disconnected, unappreciated, and attacked on the job, those feelings start to poison his body, driving him into a state of depression.[16]

> I started to get sicker and sicker due to being on heavy medications for depression and several types of mental illness. —*Computer Analyst*

> I also was diagnosed with and put on meds for really bad anxiety and depression. —*Child Welfare Worker*

At the end of this I landed in hospital for two months for treatment of major depression and anxiety. I informed management that this situation was developing almost twelve months prior, but management and HR were adamant that nothing was out of the ordinary and no policies were technically violated at any time. At the time they "gaslit" me to make me doubt I was seeing anything unusual. —*Software Engineer*

#12—PTSD

For years, post-traumatic stress disorder (PTSD) was associated with individuals exposed to long-term combat during times of war and those who endured a natural catastrophe such as a hurricane or earthquake. However, over the past decade mental health professionals have acknowledged how relentless workplace abuse can equate to significant long-term trauma in victims resulting in PTSD, sometimes referred to as Complex PTSD.

Those who suffer from PTSD endure flashbacks of the traumatic event, experience mood fluctuations, attempt to avoid people and places where the harm has occurred, and experience high levels of anxiety. Whereas the chronicle of our daily experiences is stored linearly, deep trauma is stored in the senses, carefully cataloging recollections of sounds, smells, and touch endured during the event or events. For those who suffer from PTSD, these sensory experiences are evoked in overload when the present bumps into the past, calling up these recollections in full force, causing the memories to replay in the mind's recorder as if the Creative were experiencing the original pain and destruction.[17]

> PTSD, loss of role, loss of profession, loss of confidence, loss of contacts, denigration of legacy, loss of income, loss of status. This is my life. —*General Manager*

> I have experienced workplace bullying at several places. And I believe after working as a correctional officer, I developed PTSD. I haven't worked that job in about five years or longer, and I still struggle with my trust issues in regards to my supervisor's job and my coworkers. That's not to say I don't like the people I work with, but I literally only trust two people in my office. And to be quite honest, I only trust those people I do to a very certain extent, as I inherently believe that I am truly the only person that I can trust . . . I've even watched it affect my work ethic. I eventually got to the point where I didn't care about calling in sick even though I wasn't. I even went so far as to get FMLA for

my anxiety, so that I was able to take time off even if I didn't have the paid time off accrued. —*Correctional Officer*

#13—Exclusion and Ostracization

Humans are hardwired to lean on each other for support. This propensity is likely evolutionary, for traveling alone in a dark wood opens one up to danger. In contrast, as we walk together, presenting a unified front, our collaborations outshine our individual contributions and talents. This social community builds a buffer to hardship, allowing group members to better withstand conflict and uncertainty.

To other a person, however, is the cruelest of offenses, inducing the same physical pain, according to research, as being struck. To be placed outside the circle of belonging leaves the Creative isolated and exposed, causing feelings of anxiety, doom, and exclusion.[18] In addition, over time, as the Creative is pushed closer to the corner, she begins to withdraw, no longer sharing ideas or engaging in the work community. As a result, she assigns lower ratings to her superior and institution and often initiates a job search.[19]

Schools, universities, hospitals, nonprofits, and corporations that use exclusion and ostracization as a tactic for control create a dichotomy, leading to an us versus them mentality, diminishing group trust, innovation, and productivity across the entire institution. Even if other employees are not being excluded, witnessing the pushing out of one of their own creates fear that they could be next.[20]

I worked at my school for a number of years and considered it a second home. I loved the students and parents and most of the teachers. However, there was one grade team that had a mean girl culture, everyone was scared of them but nobody would speak up. One day they set their sights on destroying me. Overnight, I went from being a beloved educator to an untouchable. Nobody would talk to me or risk being seen with me even outside of work. I was eventually driven out of a position I loved and was making a difference in. —*Educator*

#14—Medical Leave

What begins as external attacks, such as gossip, sabotage, and exclusion, slowly infests the Creative, causing her significant and extended emotional and physical suffering that prevents her from successfully completing her job responsibilities.[21] After repeated attempts to seek help from Figureheads and Human Resources, only to encounter dismissive utterances and closed doors, some Creatives are forced to take medical leave, allowing them space to heal away from the battlefield.[22]

> My biggest regret is not choosing to go on leave earlier than I did. I truly believe that the last six months I was there when the mob-bullying took place did more damage than the previous eight years combined and that was something I had neither anticipated or understood. That thick skin I'd built up vanished during those six months. It was like it was just stripped away. I still jump when a certain alert goes off on my computer, which was the same alert my work computer used to make, and I startle whenever I see vehicles which look like the company vans. —*Finance Manager*

> The Executive Director took away programs I was independently managing, because she refused to acknowledge work I was doing above my pay grade. Institutional gaslighting against me ensued, using gossip, manipulation, sabotage and exclusion tactics. I have been on medical leave from the abuse at work, suffer anxiety and panic attacks and tried to take my own life. —*Program Coordinator*

#15—Early Retirement or Disability

Targets of workplace abuse are often high producers who have enjoyed top-level success over decades in their field. They are well-liked and often sought after for advice. Therefore, when they are suddenly targeted by a Dragon who questions their expertise, removes their responsibilities, and sabotages their projects, their work life cracks and then shatters, impacting every facet of their existence.

Due to their long tenure on the job, the prospect of moving to another organization produces anxiety, especially as the need transpires amid negotiating the fallout of emotional abuse on the job. This predicament—staying in a work culture that has turned toxic or entertaining the idea of applying for a new job when emotionally and physically beaten down—leaves many Creatives with no choice but to apply for disability or seek early retirement.[23]

> After I reported them, I've been chronically mobbed, defunded, and frozen out of all departmental decision making despite having the

most seniority. I became so sick I went on leave but was forced to go back when my disability claim was denied leaving me with very little options. —*Professor*

#16—Family Strain

Victims of workplace abuse are more than employees who are being emotionally tortured on the job; they are also parents, spouses, care-takers, siblings, friends, and neighbors. Each role carries myriad responsibilities. As the toxic workplace chips away at the Creative's confidence and health, she often finds it increasingly more difficult to leave the pain and anxiety at the office door as she heads home to seek solace.[24] Consequently, the troubles at work impact her life at home, often placing strain on relationships and inhibiting her from meeting family responsibilities such as caring for aging parents or driving afternoon carpools. To fill the gap, partners must step in to help carry the load.[25]

> I spent a month in my bedroom only leaving for food and of course coffee. I cried a lot and lost my confidence. I spent a lot of time won-dering what I had done to deserve being treated and targeted this way, even though I know I am not alone in what appears to be an age old problem. Until now, I had never felt so alone, and it is only the love of my friends and family that have got me through it alive. Honestly, I am not usually a dramatic person but it stripped me of my self-esteem and trust I had in humanity. —*Emergency Management Employee*

> They recruited people against me, and I said nothing except to a few trusted confidants. I eventually decided to resign because of the strain on my family. I have a five-year-old with autism who wasn't doing well. —*Clinical Psychologist*

#17—Suicidal Ideation and Suicide

Workplace bullying is not a professional disagreement or personal-ity conflict: it is a full-frontal assault on one's humanity, poisoning the Creative's spirit, rendering him blind and mute to the outside world. The social isolation fixes his full attention on the torture, situating him in a tunnel that appears to have no way out.[26]

Psychological terrorism on the job has the potential to spur sui-cidal ideations, attempts, and completions, an outgrowth of the

Dragon's campaign to hijack the Creative's narrative, control his work environment, and ostracize him from the work community while the colleagues he once called friends silently watch the devastation.[27]

> My broker would physically and verbally abuse me to the point I attempted suicide. —*Financial Manager*

> It has affected me at times to the point of contemplating suicide. I had to be put on antidepressants and blood pressure medication. I no longer have trust for a lot of people. —*Sales Clerk*

> There are so many times when I wanted to take my own life because of what I was going through. —*Pharmaceuticals Sales Manager*

CONCLUSION

Workplace bullying is not an outside experience that a Creative encounters while going about the daily work of living. Instead, it is a full assault on her humanity, ostracizing her from a community and rewriting her script into a play where she no longer recognizes any of the characters, especially herself. This theft of the Creative's identity results in the deepest of wounds, leaving long-lasting emotional and physical suffering.

INVITATION #6

Close your eyes and envision what you looked like before the abuse. How would the people who know you best and love you most describe your character and demeanor? Now, flash forward to the shell of your identity you were left with at the conclusion of the trauma. What health consequences have you suffered? How would a bystander describe you? Compare the two identities as you think about the details of your own degradation ceremony.

Now, chart how your degradation ceremony unfolded considering the following questions:

1. How were you stigmatized (beliefs, philosophies, race, gender, sexual orientation, religion, neurodiversity, etc.)?

2. What contributed to you becoming a target (difference, boundary pushing, whistle-blowing)?
3. What was the precipitating event?
4. How did the Dragon attempt to bring you back into "compliance"?
5. What tactics did the Dragon use to assassinate your character?
6. How did the Dragon flip your script and hijack your narrative?
7. How did colleagues you considered friends turn on you?
8. Were you eventually driven out? If so, how?
9. What physical and emotional consequences did you suffer as a result of the abuse?
10. Does understanding the unfolding of the abuse, seeing similarities across Creatives' stories, help you feel less alone?

You may find it helpful to draw a circle and chart the degradation cycle visually.

Chapter 6

Reclaiming Your Narrative
Post-Traumatic Growth after Trauma

Dear Creative,

Here's a high five from me.

You are making it, and today, simply putting one foot in front of the other, is a stand up and bleacher cheer victory.

I know you are looking for the finish line, with one hand shielding your eyes like a visor, hoping to declare the win.

Here's the thing: there is no winning, for this is not a game. It is simply a state of suspension in which someone has taken your book off the shelf, drawn all over its glittery cover, and then attempted to redact your narrative, turning you into a character you don't recognize.

But try as they might, nobody gets to hijack your story; you have the sole right to your plotlines, so it's time to tell those folks to piss off.

Yes, this may sound a tad angry, but who said you don't get to be angry? When someone steals the keys to your kingdom, repaints your portrait with horns, you get to throw a bit of a tantrum, attempting to dispel the unfairness of it all and rattle the cages of those who walked with you as friends and now sit with the Dragon, nodding their heads in agreement with her fictional rewrite.

So, scream a little and give a stink eye to that woman who once broke bread with you and now seems content to watch you break your neck.

But, remember, after all of the mudslinging you have endured, there is still a window to a hopeful future that awaits you on the

other side. For the truth is, the world is still quite good and beautiful. You just got mixed up with a bad crowd. But put them in your
rearview mirror; they are no longer your responsibility, and take the
hand of that ten-year-old girl you used to be, the one who scaled the
monkey bars unafraid of falling, and launch yourself into a heck of
an act 3.

It's time to fly.

Love, Dorothy

WAITING

The sacred sleeps on the broad hips of waiting
Gentle and soft, slumbering without trepidation
Keep breathing
Your former self is just around the corner, ready to welcome you home
    again.

RISING TO INFINITY

There are some things I am going to have to let go of
Things I need to put down in order to free my heart for healing
Shame is the heaviest to hold, encompassing the full palm of my hand
A gloved compression keeps the light rays out
Bullying does that to a person
Dresses her in silks of self-accusations
The highlight reel on continuous repeat
Reliving the moments I forgot to stand up for myself
Picking up the insults catapulted my way and pinning them to my skin, as
    if they were chapters of my identity
I'm done carrying that narrative assigned to me without my permission
A script of an alternative reality that only breathes in the walls of the place
    that snuffed me out as I let my authentic self evaporate into the ether
A confirmation slip of my nothingness
Yet I am everything I was before
A full room of energies, colors mixing, ideas sprouting from my toes, too
    expansive for that office that tried to make me shrink
And so I rise despite the flogging
A small upturn in my grin that leads me back into myself and out again
    into infinity

WITNESSING

Dear Dr. Kessler,

As I sit cross-legged on the maroon sofa that makes me feel safe, I let out a discernible sigh as I read the last page of your book *Finding Meaning: The Sixth Stage of Grief*. Highlights spill across the chapters, and sticky notes dot the pages, declaring their reckoning, a reminder of all the people who have walked this path.

One line keeps asking me to open the pages and read it again: "Each person's grief is as unique as their fingerprint. But what everyone has in common is that no matter how they grieve, they share a need for their grief to be witnessed. That doesn't mean needing someone to try to lessen it or reframe it for them. The need is for someone to be fully present to the magnitude of their loss without trying to point out the silver lining."[1]

That line helped me open up, allowing me to reframe and rewrite my story without the obligation to offer gratitude to the past that contributed to my breaking. For the healing will not come by denying the pain or thanking the hurt but by remaining in the stillness, watching, waiting, and witnessing the deboning that made it impossible for me to stand.

Such insight gave me the courage to learn to walk again, in a new way, with the assistance of those I truly trust. As I rise, I use my position to stand witness to the hurt of others, knowing I don't possess the ointment required for their healing but have learned how to hold their hands as they search for it inside themselves.

This process is a relinquishment, giving up seeking reasons for the abuse, justice for the injustices, or apologies from those who will forever remain unapologetic. For there is no explanation, reparations are not forthcoming, and my C-PTSD will continue to constrict my heart at the most surprising occasions as a smell, a touch, or a sound brings me right back to her office.

Today, however, is not dependent on the confessions of another, as I lift the corner of my old self to rediscover the person I used to be. There, new sprouts whisper a greeting.

I am becoming. Again.

Sincerely, Rising

WHAT IS POST-TRAUMATIC GROWTH?

As a researcher and victim of workplace abuse trauma, I have read deep into the literature on post-traumatic growth, often inspired, and sat in a quiet, mind-numbing state watching YouTube interpretations of PTG, which unsettled me.

I think David Kessler said it best: "Your loss is not a test, a lesson, something to handle, a gift, or a blessing. Loss is simply what happens to you in life. Meaning is what you make happen."[2]

To me, this sentiment is right on. I pause when I read people's accounts of PTG in which they profess to be thankful for the abuse, the cancer, the accident, or the natural disaster because it shook them out of their old selves, revealing a more redeeming version.

However, as a narrative inquiry researcher, I believe deeply that we own our story line. If people are truly thankful for the hurt and harm they endured, I don't discount that interpretation, but I can say that my own story of workplace bullying does not elicit gratitude. I am neither appreciative nor thankful for the behavior of those who denigrated my humanity and attempted to hijack my career. No pretty bow decorates that chapter of my life marked redemption.

However, once I escaped the firing range and dragged myself to the side of the battlefield, with the help of my husband and gladiator girlfriends, I promised myself that I would dedicate my life to understanding the phenomenon of workplace bullying, listening and standing witness to the stories of those who have been abused and working to create more compassionate and innovate workspaces with guardrails—protective legislation—to hold those who bully accountable for their actions.

Inside that declaration, I have made lifelong friends through participation on the research team and executive board of the National Workplace Bullying Coalition and been inspired by my collaboration with researchers around the world through the International Association on Workplace Bullying and Harassment. I have also been deeply moved, stretched, and formed lasting connections with the hundreds of Creatives around the globe who have reached out to me wanting to tell their stories.

In this sense, my life has been enriched and blessed by these relationships, collaborations, and research partnerships that would most certainly not have transpired if not for my experience of being bullied; however, I cannot say I am grateful for the abuse, for that would give my power back to the abusers. That I am not willing to do.

I also do not subscribe to the sentiment that "everything happens for a reason," for though I enjoy a deep relationship with God, I do not believe He orchestrates disaster, terror, death, and abuse as a way to teach people a lesson or help them grow past their present circumstance. Instead, I agree with Rabbi Harold Kushner, who summed it up well, in his groundbreaking book, *When Bad Things Happen to Good People*: "In the final analysis, the question of why bad things happen to good people translates itself into some very different questions, no longer asking why something happened, but asking how we will respond, what we intend to do now that it has happened."[3]

To me, this is the crux of it all. I wasn't bullied for a divine purpose, nor were you, and spiraling down that rabbit hole will likely only leave you dizzy and in despair. But I do know that when this earth quakes, and I am dragged into its darkest crevasses, God is there holding my hand, taking what was meant to harm me and transforming it into something that brings goodness back into the world, creating hope for those enmeshed in hopelessness.

I think I have done that with my work, and I believe you have or will do it with yours. This, I believe, is where the real healing happens. You endure the abuse of broken people, behaviors that break your heart and puncture your gut, and you sit inside that pain, willing to witness the full atrocity of it all with patience, courage, and conviction. Then, over time, be it months or years, because metamorphosis can't be rushed, you take that trauma narrative, the one you didn't ask for or deserve, and you rewrite it in a way that gives you back ownership, and in that process of repossession, you use your story to help and strengthen others. To me, that is the meaning of post-traumatic growth.

THE POST-TRAUMATIC GROWTH CYCLE

I shared my own explanation of post-traumatic growth as both testimony to my healing journey and an example of the diversity of interpretations of what constitutes PTG. But there is more to the story, chapters that other researchers and Creatives have written. Everyone's truths matter.

In the mid-1990s, University of North Carolina, Charlotte, researchers Richard Tedeschi and Lawrence Calhoun began to develop a theory of why some people, following a single or prolonged trauma, such as sexual assault, a natural disaster, or the fallout of war, with time, emerge from the experience stronger and enlightened, with some even professing gratitude for the pain, calling it post-traumatic growth.[4]

In their work, Tedeschi and Calhoun delineate a five-part framework for progressing through the PTG metamorphosis.[5]

1. *First*, the victim of abuse takes his new, altered circumstances and seeks novel opportunities that honor this new life, whether it be full-time employment or volunteer efforts. For example, a victim of workplace abuse may start to advocate at the state level for protective work legislation.
2. *Second*, the victim experiences a greater sense of connection with others, prioritizing relationships over work titles and extending his social circle to include people who have suffered similar trauma.
3. *Third*, a deep introspection and inventory incurs, where the victim takes stock of his strengths, celebrating the internal fortitude that helped him fight for justice and then crawl off the battlefield to safety.
4. *Fourth*, a celebration of life prioritizes the simple, everyday gifts in his environment, eyes wide open to the sunshine as he sets off on his daily stroll.
5. *Fifth* and finally, there is a spiritual union, whether it be with a divine power or Mother Earth, in which the victim connects with something greater than himself, recognizing his pivotal place in the cosmos.[6]

In my own research, collecting more than two hundred stories from Creatives across continents, a three-part progression through the post-traumatic growth cycle emerged from the data, beginning with the prequel, followed by the seismic shift, and concluding with opting for the empowered path as a way forward. The process honors what German philosopher Friedrich Nietzsche shared in his book *Twilight of the Idols*: "What doesn't kill me, makes me stronger."[7]

The Prequel

Many of us, in the beginning, believe that our world is a beacon of possibility, filled with people driven to do good work, who when given the opportunity to act, stand on the side of goodness, fairness, and justice. We believe that our governments and institutions operate in good faith, and when difficult circumstances arise, leaders will step forward with conviction, guided by a code of ethics and human decency. We believe that hard work is rewarded, and when we show up as our best selves, ready to take care of those we are charged to serve, that disposition and dedication will be reciprocated. All of these beliefs are wrapped around each other, one over the other, like a giant ball of yarn, together encompassing what Janoff-Bulman describes as a belief in a benevolent world.[8]

The Seismic Shift

This belief serves us well, keeping our hearts soft and open, until one day a catastrophic quake, a seismic shift, repositions the ground beneath us, leaving us shaking on a landscape we no longer recognize. In workplace bullying, at this unexpected juncture, the people we trusted remove the mask and begin to act in unconscionable ways. Still clinging to the belief in a moral and just world, we reach out to the helpers—our boss's boss, the executive director, the board chair, the CEO, or perhaps Human Resources—with a trusting hand, thinking that if we share our story, that person will stand up, step out, and stop the gossip, sabotage, and exclusion that is preventing us from doing our job.

To our surprise, however, the letters we sent explaining the abuse, the documentation we attached that corroborates the story, mysteriously disappear, and in their place hangs a red sign blinking "retaliation."

Before we know it, our exclusion morphs into ostracization, and the gossip ramps up to character assassination. Suddenly the tables turn, and we are labeled the problem while the abusers clink drinks at an afternoon gathering to celebrate our annihilation.

This seismic shift divides our world into two opposing story lines, leaving us lost in a new chapter we don't recognize. Suddenly, the institution that felt like home and the colleagues we considered family have their hands on our back, pushing us toward the exit.

As the door swings shut, we are left outside in the rain, alone, watching the downpour sweep away what psychologists refer to as our assumptive self, or our predicated beliefs on how the world works. And as it circles the drain, we are overcome with a great sense of betrayal, as if we had it all wrong, and the world and its people, these people, are not at all what and who we thought they were. So, we pick up the phone to text a trusted colleague, and later follow up with a phone call, but all of our efforts at connection are met with silence.

As the rain continues to pour, washing us in shame, we have an important decision to make. Do we let go and allow ourselves to disappear into oblivion, or do we stand up, boots soaking, and take the first steps down an unmarked path in the woods, guided by faith and clinging to the hope that goodness can still be found on the other side of the forest?[9]

The Empowered Path

If we start walking away from the terror, attempting to shed the hurt, eventually we may find ourselves on the empowered path in which we rise, not because of the injuries suffered but in spite of them. In that moment, there is a reckoning, a settling and compromise of sorts: we refuse to relinquish our belief in a benevolent world, but we also recognize that our assumptive self is too damaged to be put back together again.

So, we take off our coats, shedding the old parts of our bodies that can no longer breathe, and rebuild from the bottom up, a new and stronger version of ourselves, novel, but still allowing room to accommodate our curious, former identity. It is a melding of the old with the new into a masterful creation ready to get back to work.

Now, as we look into the mirror, Kintsugi stares back at us, a concept meaning "golden journey," adapted from the ancient Japanese art of healing broken pottery with a gold lacquer that, instead of covering the cracks, accentuates the damage with a glittering glow, showing the world that the attempts to break us only made us stronger and more beautiful.[10] The golden scars now stand as a testament to the power of our healing, whispering that though we were shattered and rearranged, we are magnificently alive, redeemed, and prepared to emerge again.

WRITING AS HEALING

For me, writing offers a sort of magic, a transition to a new world, and a divine invitation to a better understanding of this one.

In my professional life, in addition to being a professor, I founded and direct the Southside Virginia Writing Project, part of the National Writing Project, a web of more than 170 sites, housed in colleges and universities, in all fifty states, the District of Columbia, the U.S. Virgin Islands, and Puerto Rico, serving more than 95,000 K–16 educators each year. That is all to say that I believe in the power of writing to change lives and alter realities. If you change your story line, you change your future.

If you were to come into my home office, you would see shelves of daybooks chronicling decades, documenting my wonderings. I only use two kinds, Miquelrius, medium size, and Leuchtturm 1917, which includes numbered pages and a table of contents. When I start a new daybook, I put my last name and the day's date on the cover and a sticker that has meaning for the moment. For example, we just returned from Jackson Hole, Wyoming, so my next notebook will be adorned with a rodeo sticker. I go through one notebook about every six weeks. I begin each entry the same way, by writing the date, exact time, and location. For example, the top of the page may say, 7/20/22, 9:17 p.m., family room.

Writing has been my salvation, and I mean that with the full power of the word. Last year, I wrote an article for the *English Journal* titled "Writing: An Act of Revolution" in which I shared:

> Today I start most mornings by writing a poem, though I seldom call myself a poet. I enjoy the way the words glide out of my experiences and fall on the page in surprising concoctions. I am always on the lookout for a story. I walk around the lake, following the goose as she chases the boy from her path. Chastising him for attempting to enter her space. I like that goose. There is a story there, a beautiful narrative. I will write about it. To do that storytelling, I need space to stretch my arms. A room where nobody will hold me down and tell me to comply. As I speak across the page, I am surprised. There is so much I don't understand about myself, corners of my kitchen I have not gotten on my hands and knees to scrub. I am trying to become. This transformation does not require advice. I am learning to narrate my life. I anxiously await the surprise. I am willing to start a revolution. Writing taught me how to do that.[11]

Writing is a teacher if you submit to the surprise, open up the deepest channels, and spill out onto the page. This writing to know and understand is especially useful when it comes to deciphering complex trauma, for when our world violently shudders, be it once as is the case of a debilitating car accident, or repeatedly, as is the experience of victims of workplace abuse, the memories of the shattering take up residence in the reptilian part of the brain, cataloged as smells, sounds, tastes, pictures, and feelings ready to activate a full-body revisit and repeat when triggered, bringing you right back to the center of the crime scene. This full immersion rerun is quite different from how typical memories are stockpiled, as a logical chronology of events, situated neatly on your mind's time line, easy to activate and decipher.

Writing, however, is an opportunity to grab onto our senses' storage, untangling the smells, sounds, tastes, pictures, and feelings, and situate them back on our story line in a narrative we can grab onto, start to make sense of, and explain to another. With each retelling of our traumatic story, whether it be a sliver or in its entirety, the mystery and pain start to dissipate, allowing us to step back into ourselves and repossess our body, reclaiming what has always been rightfully ours.

Daily writing about our pain, according to research, also creates time for deliberate rumination, in which we recount what is aching our hearts in a safe environment we control. This conscious act of re-creation provides a definitive space for making sense, lessening the unconscious brain's propensity to run the movie infinitely when we are trying to engage in our day.[12] In deliberate rumination, we set a definitive time for reflection, whether it be five or fifty minutes, and when that time ticks out, we stop the clock, reminding our brain that we are putting up the pain for the rest of the day, letting it rest on the shelf, until we pick it back up tomorrow, like a conversation with an old friend.

This process is both redemptive and healing, for research shows that people who wrote just fifteen minutes a day about the trauma they were grappling with exhibited greater mental health gains than others who wrote about topics not connected to their hurt.[13] Through this deliberate rumination, where we straighten out the mysterious squiggles of our story, we come to understand that though we can't change our time line, we can change our interpretation, as psychologist and Holocaust survivor, Viktor Frankl (1992), so aptly puts it, "When we are no longer able to change a situation, we are challenged to change ourselves."[14]

This change in our being, initiated through writing, allows us to move forward, independent of an acknowledgment of wrongdoing by our organization or an apology for the bullying from our abuser, both of which are not likely forthcoming. Writing, in this way puts us in the driver's seat of our own life, writing our story, understanding our narrative, and crafting a new plotline to carry us forward. All of this transformation is possible simply by sitting at the kitchen table, pen and paper in hand.

SIX INVITATIONS FOR REVISIONING YOUR NARRATIVE

Though everyone possesses a life's pass to writing's magic, sometimes if you are unaware of the opportunity, it is helpful to receive an invitation, a thoughtful description of what to expect if you choose to attend and engage. Below are six invitations to begin the healing journey through writing.

#1—Create a Time Line

Our brain on trauma is a scrambled entanglement of sensory overload—smells, sounds, and visions mixing together, all amplifying their part of the story. These companions, loving and well-meaning, have lost their identity, and so they make appearances at the most peculiar times, trying to make sense of the senseless. To help ground these parts of you, placing them where they belong helps you to construct a time line, the traditional kind your social studies teacher taught you back in third grade.

When I accepted this invitation, I opened my daybook to a two-page spread, drawing a horizontal line right across the middle. Then, I divided my time line into six sections, each representing a stage of the six-act play, the bullying cycle discussed in chapter 4 (target identification, jealousy and case building, the precipitating event, the underground battle, escalating attacks and mobbing, exits and cover-ups). I then labeled each section in black pen. Now that an organizing framework had been created, I filled in specific events for each stage, using different colors to help differentiate.

As you embark on this invitation, you will immediately find yourself in a mess. Embrace the chaos. Then keep doing the time line multiple times until your plotlines start to settle. It is the thinking, reorganizing, and rethinking again that lends clarity and brings healing.

#2—Third-Person Authorship: Connecting the Dots in a New Way

In narrative therapy, the person is not the problem; the problem is the problem.[15] Adopting this lens invites individuals to separate their authentic self from external struggles and hardship, opening space for a more robust and hopeful story line.

As humans navigating a complex world, early on we project story lines on ourselves and others based on thin construction. For example, if you were to look at a piece of paper made up of one hundred dots, each representing a life event, diverse plotlines fully covering the page, and then draw a line from one side of the paper to the other, interconnecting the dots on your pencil's path, you would chart one specific story map, made up of the moments you chose to highlight on your life's journey. However, with one hundred life events or dots on the paper, you could just as easily have told and reinforced a multitude of other plotlines. Therefore, sometimes the stories we tell ourselves about who we are are just one interpretation or telling.[16]

To widen our lens, viewing our time line from an alternative perspective, it can be helpful to adopt a third-person narrator, or storyteller, who recounts your bullying experience, not through your eyes but with an eagle's eye, flying high above, reporting without bias the narrative unfolding below. From this vantage point, you are you, and your problem is the problem, distinct and separate from your authentic identity.

For example, a victim dealing with the trauma of workplace abuse is not a broken person but simply a wholehearted Creative who is dealing with a Dragon. In this sense, your authentic self and the Dragon's claws are separate and distinct entities, providing you with a protective shield that prevents the Dragon from affecting your true spirit.

To help shift perspectives, write your story of workplace abuse through the lens of a third-person narrator, simply reporting on an external news story. Now look back at the reporting and notice the weightlessness that accompanies separating the bully's action from your true character. Reflect on how a third-person perspective allows you to see that the bullying was done to you but is not part of you; despite the trauma caused, you are still that same compassionate, innovative, and forward-thinking parent, partner, sibling, friend, and innovator you always were. Therefore, though the bully can inflict harm on you, she cannot become part of you. Nobody, not even the Dragon, has the power to hijack your narrative. You are the writer of your own story.

#3—What Was Violated?

We all hold values that signify what we hold sacred, guideposts for living. Michael White, an Australian therapist, social worker, and founder of narrative therapy, which honors people as the expert of their own story, describes how our internal values may impact and shape our response to trauma.

> Ongoing psychological pain in response to trauma in people's lives might be considered a testimony to the significance of what it was that those individuals held precious that was violated through the experience of trauma. This can include people's understandings about
>
> - Cherished purposes for one's life;
> - Prized values and beliefs around acceptance, justice, and fairness;
> - Treasured aspirations, hopes, and dreams;
> - Moral visions about how things might be in the world; and
> - Significant pledges, vows, and commitments about ways of being in life.[17]

For example, an administrator who always puts the needs of students first, uninterested in office politics or power, feels wounded when the superintendent implements a major initiative that plays well in the media but is unsubstantiated by research, for adoption of this new program draws significant funding away from research-backed initiatives demonstrating strong student success rates. When the administrator speaks up about the disconnect, her expertise is muted, her character assassinated, and she is pushed out of the school system, a community she dedicated herself to for more than

two decades, leaving her flailing, overcome by deep feelings of help-
lessness and shame.

As the administrator starts to explore her pain through writing,
she discovers it is not the personal attacks and loss of employment that spurred the trauma but the superintendent's violation
of her belief in servant leadership, instead putting her professional
advancement over the care of the students she was charged to uplift
and protect.

Today, write about your workplace abuse, drawing on your
time line from Invitation #1 as a resource. Next, reread your story,
attempting to take what value or values you hold dear that were
breached inside the attacks, which might include honesty, integrity,
bravery, kindness, creativity, humility, open communication, trust,
and joy. Following the identification, write another entry focused on
violation of that specific value.

#4—Identify the Moments You Held On To Who You Are

Think about one to three values you find integral to your personhood. Now reflect back on your workplace bullying experience and
identify the moments you authentically lived those values despite
the unprovoked attacks. For example, a nurse who places a high
value on compassion uncovers pockets of self-love as she recounts,
through writing, times she demonstrated deep compassion to her
patients and their families each evening on the floor despite the
gossip her nurse supervisor was spreading and the mean-spirited
jabs sent her way each time she braved the break room. Notice that
even in those moments when the Dragon attempted to hijack your
identity, you stood steadfast in your character, never abandoning
your true self and values.[18]

#5—Me in Six Months

Chronic pain, whether it be emotional or physical, over time can
cause a person to catastrophize the future, committing to the full-
throttle belief that though circumstances are dire today, tomorrow
more wreckage will occur. Such an outlook drains hope from the
future and sinks the Creative deeper into a state of hopelessness
and despair.

But what if you decided that the harm the Dragon meant for you will be transformed into opportunities to grow, prosper, and give? What if you project past today's suffering and see into the most redemptive version of your tomorrow?[19]

For example, a social worker, deeply dedicated to those in her care, is bullied out of the practice she helped to start by three women threatened by her robust client list and rave reviews online. Consequently, they launched a character assassination through office gossip, a hijacked narrative kept afloat by lies.

Though deeply wounded by the betrayal, after giving her mind and body time to heal, the social worker envisions a new story line in which she opens a private practice, in collaboration with a meditation teacher, dietitian, and another mental health professional, that specializes in helping those who have been bullied, whether at work, at home, or in a relationship. As she commits this vision to the page, it replaces all forecasts of future catastrophes.

To begin this vision of transformation, close your eyes and watch your mind's recorder as you live out your fullest life's work. With that vision harnessed, invite the narrative to stream out of you and onto the page. Some Creatives find it helpful to draw the dreamscape first or tell its story orally while digitally recording the telling.

#6—Spaceships and Unicorns

Psychological terrorism on the job will shake your confidence, leaving you desperate to steady your feet and make sense of this new reality. And as shared across the five invitations above, writing about your story, from a variety of perspectives and across diverse mediums, has great healing and redemptive power.[20] However, at times switching off the channel called reality is warranted as you prepare to transport yourself to another dimension, taking a break from the hurt and the pain.

Escape is not the same as surrender; instead, it is a battle cry of resistance, temporarily severing ties with a world that brought you down, declaring yourself an independent agent of the universe. Writer and commentator Charlie Jane Anders says it well:

> People will always try to control you by constraining your sense of what's possible. They want to tell you that reality consists of only the things that they are willing to recognize, and anything else is

foolishness. But you can reject their false limitations in the act of conjuring your own world—and carve out a pocket of your mind that they cannot touch, in the act of world-building. The more details you add to your world, the realer it feels in your mind. And thus, the better refuge it can become during hard times.[21]

Over the past several years, as part of my own healing process, I have been working on a novel that crosses the realm of the afterlife. When I am inside my writing and world building, coming to know the unexpected characters who meet me on the page, I am temporarily released from all the pressures and concerns of existence; the gap between what is and what could be makes space for me to breathe.

If you are ready to step outside your daily experience and skip into a world where everything is possible, pick up your daybook and try your hand at sketching out another dimension, where you pull the puppet strings determining the unfolding. You may find that inside your fictional writing you construct plots where characters grapple with timely challenges such as abuse and discrimination, thus playing out a narrative that reflects the challenges of today, or you may decide that you simply want to write about spaceships and unicorns, not because such creatures are metaphors for your own struggles, but simply because it makes you joyful.

So grab a pen and a glitter stick, push pause on reality, and fly into a world where you make the rules. I look forward to meeting you there.

A CEREMONY FOR REBIRTH

Ceremonies are not about the regalia and accoutrements but the formal invitation to mark a transition. They are a pause and celebration, honoring a rebirth. Ceremonial rituals provide an external metaphor for an internal change, a visual metamorphosis to a new stage. Oftentimes, however, in Western cultures, we glide through life's junctures, failing to give recognition to pivotal happenings, the dissipated energy of it all leaving us numb and lifeless.

A ceremony, however, invites a sacred pause, a space to put the experience under a microscope, zoom in on the angles that clip our heart, and then turn the corner with a concerted action, devised to guide us to a new community table.

The ceremony detailed below, adapted from the work of neuropsychologist Dr. Mario Martinez, gives the Creative a ritual to recognize the harm inflicted, noticing how its tentacles connect the abuser to the abused. Through writing and oral articulation, this bond is formally severed, regenerating the Creative's internal power that had been slowly siphoned away by the Dragon.

This ceremony provides a cushion, a soft place to land following the breakup. Such severing is not dependent on an apology, which is important, for an apology is rarely forthcoming when it concerns workplace abuse.[22]

Though Dr. Martinez's work was not specifically designed for victims of workplace bullying, the ritual offers a gateway to healing for all those whose pain is intimately tied to the intentional action of another.

The ceremony follows a three-step process:

1. *First,* identify the primary person you must formally disconnect from to cleanse your body of the toxicity of the denigration and generate new space for grace and healing.
2. *Second,* write a letter to the Dragon (or Community Builder or Shapeshifter) announcing your intention to officially disconnect. To formalize the process, I find it helpful to write the letter on personal stationery. It may sound something like this:

Dear Tina,

This letter serves as notice of my formal disconnection from you and this organization. I will no longer allow you to denigrate my character, and I will no longer stand witness to your actions that are not in keeping with my values and ethical code of conduct. You no longer have power over me, and I no longer have an obligation to you. These words serve as the formal severing of our relationship.

Sincerely, Self-Respect

3. *Third,* light a candle, read the letter aloud, and then hold it over the flame as the universe reclaims the pain, giving you back the authorship of your life.

In summary, writing is an external act that connects us to our internal experience, creating space to record our stories and reclaim our narratives. The simple act of putting pen to paper serves as a declaration of who we are and what we have lived through. Writing every day invites us to claim our identity on paper and remind ourselves and others that we own our story, and our story matters.

CONCLUSION

The deep trauma that emerges inside a Creative during and following workplace bullying is not a result of the harsh words and revoked invitations, though certainly, those experiences hurt, but the Dragon's attempt to rename who they are, redact what they have accomplished, and edit out their intentions. This hijacking of their personal story is intended to obliterate their existence. This annihilation not only affects their sense of self but shatters their assumptions of fair play and a benevolent world, making their entire life philosophies quake and disappear. Apologies and reparation are rarely forthcoming, so Creatives must attempt to heal themselves. In the absence of statements of regret from the abusers, writing is one way for Creatives to make sense of their new realities and claim who they are on the page. In this sense, writing is not a lonely act but an attempt at a personal revolution.

INVITATION #7

Now that you have accepted some or all of the invitations above, step outside yourself and create space to stand witness to the struggle of another. Hold that space without offering a silver lining or advice. Instead, momentarily hold another person's pain, treating it as sacred. Later, reflect in your daybook how listening to the hardship of another, whether it be a victim of workplace abuse or another trauma, without trying to fix it or make it better had transformative power, letting the person know her experience is tragic, her feelings are valid, and her story is sacred.

Chapter 7

Characteristics of Creative Cultures

CREATIVITY IS

I know you've taken it in the teeth out there, but the first guy through the wall—he always gets bloody. Always. It's the threatening of not just the way of doing business, but in their minds, it's threatening the game. But really what it's threatening is their livelihoods. It's threatening their jobs. It's threatening the way that they do things. And every time that happens, whether it's the government or a way of doing business or whatever it is, the people who are holding the reins—have their hands on the switch—they go batshit crazy. —*Boston Red Sox owner John Henry from the movie* Moneyball[1]

I love this quote. It is such a good reminder that as Creatives, we really do take it in the teeth. For if you think big and muster the courage to say, "Hey, what would you think if we tried something new?," you'd better lean against the wall, steady yourself, and prepare for an onslaught of resistance, knowing they will go "batshit crazy."

It's the Creative's conundrum: do you adjust your accent, select your words carefully, and speak the company mantra, even inside those moments of deep discernment, when you know they simply have it all wrong? Or do you raise your hand, propose something different, and hope that a brave and innovative soul in the audience is willing to stand up, too? Because here's the thing: I have yet to find an organization that does not have Creatives, oozing with ideas, eager to disrupt the common story. However, what does happen, with alarming frequency, is that these seekers witness first-hand the fallout of those who dare to be different, so they retreat, go underground, clothe themselves in the everyday instead of inviting their elusive tomorrow to shine.

So, what do you do if you find yourself in an organization that requires you to play small and use muted colors? Perhaps it is an institution with a legacy of stagnation and fear-based leadership, or maybe it's a company with a history of a creative culture, but new management has squashed those big thoughts.

From my own research and experience, supported by the research of others, the best advice I have—and you will not like it—is to leave. As a young academic, my dear friend and mentor Jane Hansen advised me to create a vita full of publication, presentations, and diverse experiences that always allows me to walk. Each year, I pass that same insight onto my college students, to craft a career that is not handcuffed to an institution but, instead, possesses an infinite number of doors and windows open to new possibilities.

I believe in identifying the work you feel called to do and then become consummately loyal to it. Sometimes that stance charges you to break with an organization or change how you show up and interact with an institution. More important, it insists that you live inside your values, not betray who you are for a place that really doesn't want you.

But what exactly is creativity, and what characteristics do creative cultures share?

WHAT IS CREATIVITY?

The definitions of creativity are as infinite as the concept itself, but I think David Perkins's Snowflake Model and Robert Sternberg's Investment Theory help to get us to a deeper understanding.

Creative environments are not constructs of brick and mortar, though certainly innovative layouts help to spur collaboration and invite time for quiet contemplation. Instead, creative cultures emanate out of the habits of creative people, and the environment simply needs to avoid impeding their work. The bar is quite low. However, I can't tell you how many organizations I have sat inside and heard about through my interviews that spend a great deal of time talking about innovation but very little time innovating.

Creativity, however, does not live in the talking points or the press releases; it comes alive in the messy complexity of doing the work.

So, what creative work are these innovators doing?

According to Perkins's Snowflake Theory, Creatives possess a high tolerance for and may even consciously seek out complexity and disorder, recognizing that the new is only possible inside the chaos. They also hone the skill of finding questions, understanding that inquiries are far more interesting than answers and that the type of questions you ask shape the scope and reach of your discoveries. In other words, ask big, get big.

In addition, Creatives are not held down by the dictum of the day. Instead they maintain a fluidity of thought and a belief in the metamorphosis of understandings, charging them to question tradition and push past status quo thinking. Creatives are also risk takers, unafraid of failure, enlivened by working on the edge, knowing that the collapse is simply part of the building process.

Their propensity to push boundaries charges Creatives to seek out contrarians; they want their ideas questioned, notions stretched, and holes poked in their findings, believing in the necessity of multiple perspectives and critical conversations in breaking new ground.

Finally, Creatives' motivations live on the inside, charging them to compete with themselves. They are in the game not to beat their opponent but for the pure joy of invention. This internal calibration they use to determine success can make Creatives difficult to control, for they don't require outside validation to produce and perform.[2]

As a writer, I appreciate Don Murray's contention that speaks well to creative work:

> The writers of such drafts must be their own best enemy. They must accept the criticism of others and be suspicious of it; they must accept the praise of others and be even more suspicious of it. They cannot depend on others. They must detach themselves from their own page so they can apply both their caring and their craft to their own work.[3]

Perkins's Snowflake Theory partners well with Sternberg's Investment Theory, in which Creatives buy low and sell high, committing to explore obscure or sometimes unpopular ideas, shaking the unwritten rule books of their organizations, which can make them targets of workplace abuse. As Csikszentmihalyi (1996) shared, "being alone at the forefront of a discipline also makes you exposed and vulnerable. Eminence invites criticism and often vicious attacks.

When an artist has invested years in making a sculpture, or a scientist in developing a theory, it is devastating if nobody cares."[4]

Organizations, however, that are willing to sit in the discomfort, as they explore new territory, position themselves to reap the rewards of "selling high" when they come out victorious on the other side of exploration, leading their industry into new possibilities.[5]

Welcome to the professional development that never happened. Today our experts will share advice on identifying, withstanding, and eliminating workplace bullying.

CHARACTERISTICS OF CREATIVE CULTURES

As shared earlier, as part of my process of collecting stories across the world from victims of workplace abuse, I posed two essential questions or requests. The first invited Creatives to share the story of a time they were bullied on the job; the second, to tell a story of an environment or culture they have participated in that encouraged creativity and intellectual risk taking.

Participants responded with vigor. For the most part, the institution where the bullying occurred usually was different from the institution that encouraged creativity and intellectual risk taking. However, at times, an organization spurred innovation for decades, but due to a management change, sank back into tradition, enforcing hierarchies that kept people in their lanes. This type of radical change demonstrates how a shift in leadership can sink an organization into complacency or catapult it into new visions of innovation.

As I read and reread through the hundreds of pages of narratives, coding the data, categories emerged that were later collapsed into themes. Across people's stories, eleven practices or conditions floated up as characteristic of creative environments. Below, I share a brief description of each partnered with the voice of participant storytellers.

#1—Practice Transparent Decision Making

Transparency is really about trust and telling the truth. Organizations that openly share thought processes behind decision making, reflections on mistakes made, and equity data such as salaries paid across departments invite open discussions and debate. These critical conversations are possible because secrets are not locked in the closet but, instead, information is openly shared at the boardroom table, inviting diverse perspectives to the discussion. Unfortunately, when information is kept hidden, such as how much people are paid and what opportunities for advancement are available, it creates a closed-circle culture, establishing clearly delineated ingroups and outgroups, perpetuating inequalities and stagnation. Such cultures provide fertile ground for Dragons.[6]

> Previously, I have worked in an open and transparent culture. One of encouragement, sharing of ideas, risk-taking and developing oneself and team members within the profession of education. For example, in a previous role I created a department of advanced practitioners and led staff development across the college. —*Senior Manager*

#2—Extend Autonomy and Trust

Creatives have a wide wingspan, requiring significant space to stretch and take flight. Control is helpful during the interview and hiring process, but once onboarded, peak performance and innovation require supervisors to trust the expertise of the Creatives they hired, encouraging them to fly.[7] When Creatives are given autonomy, they perceive the freedom as a reflection of their organization's belief in their ability to do good work. Consequently, their dedication to the organization increases, and their propensity to engage in the intellectual risk taking required of innovation expands.[8] Inside this win-win scenario, students, patients, and clients receive more individualized and compassionate care, and institutional problems are addressed and ready to be solved.

> The employer had full trust and confidence in my abilities and allowed me to make all purchasing decisions and to determine which titles we would sell in all of our stores. —*IT Professional*

> I was an art teacher when I began teaching. I had complete autonomy over my curriculum. I was allowed to explore many subjects and methods with students. My independence influenced my rapport with students in a positive way. —*Art Teacher*

When I was working for a tech company in Research and Development, I had several mentors there who allowed me to develop and take ownership of the design and experiment projects. —*Electrical Engineer*

#3—Give People a Voice

Turning back the pages of history, surely wars might have been avoided and people could have been healed by the hands of a Creative who saw the solution but was forced into silence, causing everyone to lose. When Creatives are not able to speak their truth, share their ideas, or engage in complex conversations, their voices begin to shrink. Over time, they become so small as to be almost indiscernible; even their inner soul can barely make out the whisper. However, when critical conversations are encouraged, deep emotions are channeled into building solutions instead of being relegated to office storage.[9]

In silencing cultures, innovations set out in search of more open spaces, leaving ethical violations to multiply. Cultures that insist on a single plotline, editing out all opposition, are far more likely to turn a blind eye to bad behavior, as is the experience of whistle-blowers. For contrary to popular belief, employees do not leak confidential information to the press for personal gain or notoriety. In contrast, they only let the story line spill following numerous failed attempts at appealing to upper management to speak up for justice, a brave act that almost always results in immediate retaliation, egregious bullying, and job loss.[10]

I was not afraid to give my point of view or to raise issues that concern me and my work. My input was seen as valuable and I was encouraged to bring new ideas on board. —*Event Coordinator*

When I worked in a healthy environment my work was supported and my knowledge was sought after. I felt valuable and healthy. —*Professor*

So, as long as I have a chance to have a voice and to express myself in a professional manner without censure, I'm satisfied. —*Teacher*

#4—Play on Employees' Strengths

In the classroom and in the schoolyard, children are often encouraged to be well rounded, prompting caregivers to keep an eye out for their weaknesses and commit to building them up. This strategy, however, is not always the best approach. For example, in the workplace, employees who are encouraged to play to their strengths are more productive, confident, and engaged, positioning them to expand to the fullest, understanding that their passion and talent are boundaryless.[11] Organizations that encourage Creatives to commit to projects that make their hearts flutter with excitement and anticipation also experience lower burnout rates, for it is usually not the load carried that burns out the candle but the room in which the candle is forced to burn.[12]

> Prior to the merge, I was blessed with a cohesive team, a visionary leader who believed in me, and was able to stretch, grow, make positive changes. I created new programs and felt I was always learning. My heart was open to connect with clients and colleagues and I loved my work. The culture was one of amplifying strengths, giving people respect and autonomy to deliver their best with flexibility to pursue other life goals and continue personal growth, which was greatly valued by the CEO. —*Caretaker for Adults with Disabilities*

> My first full time job, where I worked for seven years, was in a school where everyone's experience and opinion was listened to. Responsibilities were given based on people's interests and talents and everyone was encouraged to grow and take risks. —*Teacher*

#5—Provide Positive Feedback and Celebrate Success

We do not escape report cards when we leave the walls of school, for on the job evaluations continue to play a pivotal role in determining how we work. A barrage of "you should have done it this way" can start to weigh heavily on a Creative, preventing him from venturing into new territory for fear of rebuke. Constant negativity is a paradox of sorts, making the Creative feel constantly under the microscope yet completely insignificant.

However, when a Creative receives positive feedback, detailing the parts of his project that elicited a high-five, energy streams through his body, resulting in a momentary feeling of invincibility. Inside that energized space, the Creative decides to exceed himself, growing in directions he'd labeled dormant. Such feeling is amplified as the crowd cheers, knowing that his individual win is a victory for the larger community.[13]

My current boss and workplace is so supportive. I am thriving and getting back to creating innovative solutions with stakeholders. I am getting such positive feedback. I jump out of bed now to get to work! —*Community Development*

The VP of the instructional designers held regular meetings just to discuss design theories and share ideas and challenges and celebrate really great outcomes. —*Instructional Designer*

One Ph.D. material scientist was particularly impressed with my work, and she was the one who taught me how to use the equipment and then showed me that I was actually the most accurate at reading the spectrum. It was great to be rewarded with praise for doing a job well. —*Electronic Engineer*

#6—Engage in Courageous Problem Solving

We often work under the assumption that people don't like problems, purporting that work is a place where employees would prefer to dodge the mess. When it comes to the Creative, however, that argument breaks down. For it is not the tangle that frustrates the Creative, but the complacency in addressing it. To a Creative, problems are not roadblocks but energizers, offering opportunities to dive into the complexity of an issue, pull the loose strings, and test solutions whose implementation helps better support the students, patients, and clients he is called to serve. To do that work, the Creative requires room to iterate, understanding that failure is always an option, and a breakdown in one solution is simply an invitation to try out another. In this sense, problems are the best mechanism to foster engagement, for they continually pull the Creative back to the table, nourishing his curiosity.[14]

At my previous school, we wrote a grant to create an integrated curriculum around Social Studies and Science. We worked every year to improve what we were doing, evaluate what went well, what could go better, and figure out how to help students deepen their thinking, creating their own solutions to environmental problems. It was so fulfilling. —*Teacher*

#7—Encourage the Creation of Something New

Copy machines and reprints drain the life from the Creative who yearns to make something new, for exhilaration accompanies creating a product, designing a program, or planning an event that will solve problems, educate, or simply bring joy to a community. The act of creation opens up all of the windows in the room and expands what is possible. When the Creative has an opportunity to make instead of duplicate, she becomes fully engaged in the work, seeing her role inside the organization's mission, her senses fully ignited.[15]

> I always valued what my colleagues contributed and often let them create the new system we would use or provide input into new policy we would implement. It definitely wasn't my way or the highway!! It was a team working together and respecting each other. —*Car Parts Delivery Correspondent*

> Together we created an emergency preparedness infographic/pictograph for older adults and wheelchair users. Our work was a finalist for a national award and used as a model for other designs. It was a very iterative process as we got early drafts into the hands of the intended end users. We have now shared our ideas in academic papers. —*Community Developer*

#8—Invite and Support Intellectual Risk Taking

Though there is a comfort in sliding into the steady zone, knowing what is ahead, each day following a predictable cadence, for the Creative, the monotony of it all heightens her dissatisfaction at work, leaves her prone to disengagement, and often prompts her to seek out more innovative cultures that will help her grow. For the Creative to stay and flourish, she needs to walk on the edge, the path where falling is highly possible but leads to views and opportunities only available for those who take the risk. The Creative is up on current research, understands the competition, and sees the holes in the future that nobody has attempted yet to fill. When given the space and resources to innovate, she creates products and processes that allow her organization to soar.[16]

> Working at the Writing Center, I would use creative ideas & take risks on new ideas to figure out how to best inform a student on how to complete a task. —*Writing Tutor*

I was surprised that the men (also aircraft mechanics) supported me and each other intellectually. —*Licensed Aircraft Mechanic*

I am part of a group of creative people and we support and encourage each other as we learn new skills with new technologies. —*Shop Assistant*

#9—Encourage Respect and Collaboration across Disciplines and Departments

The construct of unbiased reporting is both a falsehood and impossibility, for regardless of our openness to grow, our view of the world is filtered through our life experiences, straining out important parts we never see. Those filters include our cultural background, educational experiences, books read, discussions had, and content area expertise.

Without knowing it, we move through life in our own lane, finding it unsettling to take a parallel or intersecting path. The problem with this route, however, is that there is so much we don't see or understand, experiences available to us if just walked across the street. To combat her limited vision, the Creative consciously seeks out connections with those who are different. This diversity in experiences and perspectives widens the field of vision, inviting a collaborative group to approach problems from different directions and depth. As a result, the research, products, and designs are more inclusive and innovative. In addition, because the tent is big, it is not just the Creative sharing her work but a team of people, each from a different community, linked together by this one project, resulting in a vastly extended reach.[17]

I am currently re-designing a process that was previously entirely in-house and making it a partnership between our department and an outside vendor who can complete tasks in which we are not experts (ie, we are all writers and fundraisers, but part of this task requires graphic design and layout). The cost of having an outside vendor complete the work rather than consuming staff time with something at which we're not skilled is a more creative use of our staff resources. —*Administrative Staff Member at a College*

Another site I work at, in the same organization, respects the individual physical needs of Sonographers to create their images. If you need equipment in another space or angle, you move it. There is no territorial aggression, no gossip about how you position things, no subtle manipulation of float pool staff to teach them how not to position equipment. —*Ultrasound Tech*

#10—Offer Meaningful, Deep, and Relevant Professional Development

Learning a new skill is like rebirth, an opportunity to recalibrate and start over. In school, if we are lucky, we learn beside inspirational teachers vested in our growth and development. However, once we enter the larger world of work, often those opportunities to outgrow ourselves become scant, paralyzing us in our current position and stifling our chances for upward mobility. Or sometimes, as is often the case for teachers, professional development feels like riding a perpetual merry-go-round, one new class after the other, each one pushing a new initiative, the agenda ever-changing, all demanding more of a schedule already overflowing.

A happy medium is possible between letting learning go dormant and taking a tennis ball launcher approach, in which a manager hurls learning opportunities scattershot from every direction, overwhelming all those in its path. That sweet spot is personalized learning, where the Creative is invited to seek out opportunities to deepen his skills and knowledge base in areas that directly relate to his job and speak to his passions. This professional development is ongoing, providing the Creative with a team of co-learners negotiating new territory together for an extended period of time.[18]

> I was the chair for three years and invited faculty to try out new ideas with course development, workshops, activities, new assignments, research, conference attendance-all supporting funding. We created and revised several courses and conducted numerous workshops. The best response I had from a professor during her annual review, as I had listed all of the creative challenges she had engaged in, was that she felt really seen, heard and valued. —*Professor*

#11—Be Driven by Purpose

Many people trudge through the nine-to-five, giving a fist pump on hump day and a sad sigh as Sunday dinner concludes and the work week beckons. The Creative is different. She shows up to her job, not to check a box or fulfill a requirement, but because she deeply believes in the work, driven by purpose and mission. The Creative adopts a spirituality about her role; she refers to it as a calling or an inner force driving her to new explorations. The Creative is innately curious and driven to serve people, causes, or larger global issues; therefore, in order for her to commit to sticking around, she must believe the institution is authentically devoted to the cause and that it is possible for her to fulfill parts of her life mission by showing up each day.[19]

> Most of what I do involves creativity. Besides instructing from a method book written to be used in mixed instrumental classes, I am always on the look-out for students who could be assigned additional performance opportunities for solo work and small ensemble partici- pation. I pursued these opportunities knowing that I would not receive monetary compensation. I simply feel called to help kids. —*Band Director*

So, taking the eleven constructs above, what can an organization do to create a fertile ground where creativity sprouts and multiplies? It is far simpler than we make it. The answer resides in opening up space for people to tell their story, share their opinion, and ask for what they need. How do you do that work? A creativity audit is a great place to start.

THE CREATIVITY AUDIT: STEPS ORGANIZATIONS CAN TAKE TO HEAL AND GROW THEIR CULTURE

Most organizations have two cultures that exist in parallel universes but never intersect. One culture is described in the employee hand- book and splashed across social media; the other is the culture that insiders experience. This second culture is not a secret or an enigma, but it is discussed openly in backchannel texts between colleagues forced to endure long administrative meetings filled with celebrations, announcements, and reviews of bureaucratic policies but devoid of deep discussion of the critical issues affecting the institution.

These inside conversations rarely make it to the outside because managers and administrators often craft structures that only give hand claps and pats on the back space to breathe. Such environ- ments spread toxic positivity, promulgating the voices of those reso- lute to staying on message while stifling Creatives, who are quickly labeled contrarians simply because they ask the big questions that push back the walls.

So, how do you break through the facade and bring the backchannel conversations to the main stage? A creativity audit is a useful place to start. Begin by crafting an anonymous online survey tool that invites colleagues to provide feedback on the previously discussed eleven constructs or a slimmed down, individualized version that speaks to the values of the culture you are trying to create. Next, review the data and find corners where the organization is falling down on the job.

For example, do the majority of employees feel cross-collaboration is discouraged, and that they seldom have a voice in decision making related to their work? If so, craft an open call for a group of people who would like to dive into the cultural structures that need to be changed or created in order for those two opportunities to arise. Then have the employees who worked on the initiatives, not the leaders or managers, report their findings and engage the group in a larger discussion on next steps needed. It can be overwhelming to eat an elephant over a single lunch, so it is wise to focus on one or two constructs at a time.

Most important, once an organization commits to hearing colleagues' voices and enacting suggested changes, it is imperative that the organization follow through. Nothing is more disheartening than putting your full efforts into a project only to have the results viewed as insignificant and incomplete, and then shelved. Once simple changes are enacted, keep checking to see how it is going. Much of this work, therefore, is not about moonshot accomplishments but simply creating a two-way highway for people to share ideas, exchange perspectives, and collaboratively reshape a culture that invites all people to thrive.

CONCLUSION

Creativity is an open field where people gather to work, play, and exchange ideas about projects that speak to their passions and advance the mission. The magic is not in the pool table or catered lunches, though such amenities certainly may bring joy and appreciation, but in the sacred promise to offer transparency in decision making, a voice for all people, the space to stretch and fly, the solitude to think, the backroads to engage in cross-collaboration, the expectation to offer and receive fruitful feedback, and the encouragement to take intellectual risks in a pursuit of trying something new that plays to employees' strengths and the organization's mission. And, voilá! In this atmosphere, something revolutionary transpires, something that was always living within the walls. It simply needed an invitation to emerge.

INVITATION #8

Begin by rewinding the tape to childhood and replaying an experience where you were engaged in your work full-throttle, whether the setting be a sandbox, a neighborhood park, or a soccer field. Then stretch out that moment like a piece of chewing gum, capturing all of the intricacies that made you feel alive. Now go back with a pen or a highlighter, and notate the constructs that made those moments possible, such as the gift of freedom or the space to yell and scream who you are. Then fast-forward to your adult life and discover new moments where your creativity reigned, considering again the constructs that invited the experience.

Now transport yourself to your current workplace and considering whether it is an environment that makes you feel alive, charged by the prospect of possibilities. If in your current work environment your heart isn't in it, what constructs do you require to get back the beat? Are such changes possible in your current position, or is a change in order? If it's time to switch paths, describe the type of setting you require, narrowing it down to your non-negotiables.

Next, as you launch your search, resist the urge to seek out job titles. Instead, explore new spaces that inhabit the characteristics that make you come alive. It just might land you in a place, an industry, or in an area of the world that has been waiting for you for decades but not until today were you willing to open the invitation and accept the new adventure.

Chapter 8

Closed Circles and Big-Tent Belonging

A Theory of Workplace Abuse

THE TENT

There is a tent out back
It has always been there
Set up by Welcome
And maintained by Infinity
There is no passcode
The sides are open
Anyone may enter
A skylight is cut from the top
The sun shines in

As a narrative inquiry researcher on a quest to understand the phenomenon of workplace bullying, I am immersed in the stories of Creatives who have been abused on the job.

In addition to the hundreds of Creatives who have participated in my research study, each week others who have stumbled upon my research site or read one of my articles in *Psychology Today* reach out via email, sharing their plotlines, attempting to make sense of the grenade planted in their office closet, detonated unexpectedly, blowing up their career, sense of fair play, and belief in a benevolent world.

Though workplace bullying as a field of study is still relatively new, the research is building, lending insight into cultures that tolerate and sustain hurt. The list of researchers and institutions that have contributed to the literature on workplace abuse is vast. The following offers a small peek, just a glimmer of impactful

139

Chapter 8

contributors; consequently, many significant researchers have been left out of the story unfolding here. For a deeper dive, I encourage you to check out *Bullying and Harassment in the Workplace: Theory, Research, and Practice.*[1]

A BRIEF PRIMER ON THE RESEARCH'S EVOLUTION

The study of workplace bullying began in earnest during the early sixties, with Konrad Lorenz, a Nobel laureate who studied aggression in animals, noting that birds in particular, when feeling threatened, will join forces with feathered conspirators and fly combatively toward a victim targeted for elimination. Though one bird may be considered pugnacious, the mob escalates the pecking to a war. Lorenz later connected his findings to playground aggression in children and then to workplace abuse.[2]

In the eighties, the German-born Swedish citizen, psychologist Heinz Leymann, revolutionized the field, demonstrating the detrimental impact workplace bullying has on both victims and organizations.[3] To further cement that foundational work, in the early nineties Ståle Einarsen at the Bergen Bullying Research Group, University of Norway, Bergen, developed the Negative Acts Questionnaire, which continues to be the gold standard self-reporting tool for collecting information on workplace bullying.[4] Building on that momentum, in the late nineties Ken Westhues, a sociology professor at the University of Waterloo in Ontario, shone the spotlight on workplace bullying in higher education.[5]

Around that same time, Noa Davenport, Ruth Schwartz, and Gail Elliott published their seminal book, *Mobbing: Emotional Abuse in the American Workplace*, highlighting the phenomenon for the American workers; and psychologists Ruth and Gary Namie founded what would later become the Workplace Bullying Institute, which conducts research, assists victims, and educates organizations and unions.[6]

In 2010, the National Workplace Bullying Coalition was founded in the United States with the mission to eliminate workplace bullying through education, support, and advocacy.[7] Several years later, Maureen Duffy, a family therapist specializing in trauma-informed care, and Len Sperry, a professor of mental health and counseling, coauthored two leading books in the field, *Mobbing: Causes,*

Consequences, and Solutions and *Overcoming Mobbing: A Recovery Guide for Workplace Aggression and Bullying.*[8] Together, these books present an integrative picture of workplace terror, examining the intersecting impact on individuals, groups, and organizations.

Last, the parallel and sometimes intersecting field of psychopathy is led by Dr. Robert Hare, author of *Without Conscience: The Disturbing World of Psychopaths among Us.*[9] Hare later applied his study of psychopathy, much of which was conducted in prisons, to the boardroom, examining work cultures that attract, hire, and promote "successful" psychopaths and these predators' impact on the health of individuals and organizations. Hare later partnered with his colleague Paul Babiak, an industrial organizational psychologist, to share that research in the book *Snakes in Suits: When Psychopaths Go to Work.*[10]

However, despite the expanding field of workplace bullying, definitive theories remain scant. For though we can identify the symptoms, measure the impact, and name the cultural characteristics of organizations that tolerate and, at times, encourage abusive and unethical behavior, the why of it all remains somewhat nebulous for Dragons rarely openly self-identify as predators, and their slippery relationship with the truth makes them unwilling and unreliable narrators.

Therefore, as a survivor of workplace bullying and a student of story, over the years I have begun to develop a theory of workplace bullying, grounded in narrative and built on the theme of belonging, called closed circles versus big-tent belonging.

Though I toyed with the idea of starting our journey together with this theory, I saved it for the last act, discerning that without a deep exploration of the characters and plotlines of workplace abuse, it would be difficult to fully conceptualize.

CLOSED CIRCLES VERSUS BIG-TENT BELONGING: A THEORY OF WORKPLACE ABUSE

What speaks most to me about stories is not the surface acts, where the action unfolds, but the deeper themes that whisper insights into the complex world around us. When it comes to workplace bullying, I believe that the primary theme is set firmly on the construct of belonging. However, where the plotlines become devastatingly interesting is in how the leading characters interpret, strive for, maintain, and at times weaponize the concept of being part of a group. Let's dive into the theory.

Interpret Belonging

As writers, in our mind's eye we sit with our fictional characters, watching their morning routines, workday interactions, and evening drinks with friends. Though few of these scenes will survive to wiggle into our story, the time spent dedicated to the task invites us to become researchers of our characters, exploring them in their natural habitat and giving insight into how they interpret what it means to belong. Does our main character send out an office-wide email, inviting all to the corner pub after work, or does he whisper the planned gathering to a strategic group of insiders, intending to spend the evening plotting?

Studying Dragons and Creatives, though real people, is not so different from examining fictional characters, for understanding their beliefs, values, and conflicts opens a window to how they interpret the construct of belonging.

Beliefs

The Dragon hoards her riches, self-nominates for recognition, and makes sure only one chair is at the head of the table. Her belief in the world is grounded in scarcity, where only a few gold stars are awarded, making fight-to-the-death competitions mandatory. In contrast, the Creative spies the expansive ocean of abundance, understanding that her flame burning brightly is not diminished by lighting that of a colleague.

To the Dragon, who views outsiders as a looming threat to her finite power, belonging must be controlled and hoarded. The Creative, however, believes in the power of infinite numbers, inspired by the multitude of opportunities around her, understanding that belonging is not an award bestowed on a chosen few but an inherent birthright for all.

Values

The Dragon values power and compliance. Her Shapeshifters and Community Builders must flatter her, sleeping at her feet as they await their next directive. The Creative, on the other hand, sees autonomy and exploration as essential components of innovation, requiring vast space to try out different strategies, at times calling on unorthodox methods to get the job done.

For the Dragon, in order to belong, you must obey her rules with full devotion, whereas the Creative invites colleagues to venture off on their own in search of new discoveries, knowing that while parts of their journey will be solitary, the health of an expansive community rests on supporting the uniqueness of each individual.

Conflict

For the Dragon, the conflict is external. Those who play outside the closed circle and shake up the hierarchy as they go about solving long-standing problems, threaten the Dragon's single plotline, where she is the puppeteer, manipulating the strings. For the Creative, the conflict is internal, charging her to live according to her own values and measure success against her own determinants. The Creative competes with herself, possessing no desire to clip the wings of colleagues. She is driven by a larger purpose, inspired by the divine, and does not look to the outside to validate her self-worth.

Whereas the Dragon's and Creative's beliefs, values, and conflicts create contrasting interpretations of belonging, the way in which they strive to form community also presents quite differently. The Dragon creates a closed circle of confidants while the Creative erects a tent, with open sides, where everyone is invited to belong to the community while still fully belonging to themselves.

Strive for Belonging

As seasoned storytellers, we come to understand that reality is fluid; it depends on the lens and interpretation of the teller. Because the Dragon and the Creative assign vastly different meanings to the construct of belonging, the way in which they strive to establish community also takes opposing paths. The Dragon follows the signs marked "closed circles" whereas the Creative dances toward the path marked "big tent."

I use the term closed-circle belonging to describe how the Dragon maintains power and exerts control by constructing a small inner circle of colleagues, compelled by tight group norms, that she charges to carry out her dirty work. To stay inside the circle, Shape-shifters and Community Builders must commit to hating the same people and enforcing compliance. If, at any time, a member of the closed circle questions the Dragon, exhibits thoughts that challenge the status quo, or begins to socialize outside the group, that person will be immediately expelled.

In contrast, big-tent belonging is predicated on the notion of abundance and deep thought. Big-tent belonging has no definitive boundaries, and all are welcome at the table. Diverse thoughts are present, and challenges are encouraged, for Creatives believe that our difference builds possibilities and nurtures discoveries. No tests or norms are required to be part of this group; members are simply encouraged to think big, listen hard, and work toward the larger mission with enthusiasm, compassion, and transparency.

The Dragon's commitment to drawing a closed circle, governed by strict group norms and exclusionary practices, is at odds with the Creative's propensity to pitch a big tent, where everyone is welcome and ideas flow freely. This contrast creates a conflict as the two ways of striving for community bump up against each other, producing fertile ground for workplace abuse.

Maintain Belonging

Once the Dragon closes her circle, and the Creative invites everybody in, they must maintain their constructions of belonging using diverse tools, establishing unique settings, and taking contrasting approaches to resolving conflicts.

Tools

The Dragon uses humiliation and belittlement, gossip, smear campaigns, exclusion, sabotage, gaslighting, ostracization, and retaliation to protect her closed circle's perimeter.

In contrast, to sustain the big tent's infinite membership, the Creative encourages her comrades to wander freely under its cover while conversing across departments and specialties, allowing them to experience the sense of safety that emerges when one realizes she does not need to change who she is in order to be part of the group. This acceptance spurs her to take the intellectual risks required for great discoveries and engage in deep reflection as she measures her progress. And if she falters, as we all are guaranteed at times to do, she leans on her big-tent colleagues, who graciously offer the empathy needed to reboot her resolve and ready herself to set out on the creative path again.

Setting as Third Teacher

In storytelling, settings are integral to the plotline, for they provide a backdrop and context that ground the narrative in time and place. However, when it comes to workplace bullying, the setting is more than a landscape, it takes on the role of a third teacher, helping to maintain, instruct, and establish the cultural environment.

As an educator by trade, I borrowed the term "third teacher" from the Reggio Emilia approach to learning, in which the environment is seen as a central instructor and guide to the authentic learning process.[11] Although the ethos of workplace bullying is opposite the innately joyful Reggio classroom, this groundbreaking idea of the environment as a central instructor is a powerful driving force in the bully war, with its contrasting interpretations of belonging.

Though poor decision making and incivility make their appearances in most organizations, for workplace abuse to transpire, the setting must be ripe for terror. Such backdrops tend to enforce a strict hierarchy, homogeneous thinking, conflict-avoidant communication, a lack of constructive feedback, and blame and shame responses to problems. Most important, Figureheads, such as C-suite executives, boards of governors, executive directors, and other top-ranked employees with significant spheres of influence, must fail to listen to, guide, and help victims of workplace bullying who, after exhausting all other resources for support and protection, reach out to them for help in their quest to maintain their belonging.

In contrast, when the setting is full of windows and stairs, inviting people to look in all the corners and travel up and down the hierarchy to solve complex problems, Creatives thrive. Inside autonomous decision making and cross-collaboration, Creatives become problem solvers, intellectual risk takers, and change agents in their community, their actions and accomplishments serving as a third teacher for onlookers trying to decide if it is safe to jump.

Efforts to Resolve Conflicts

Stories that capture your heart, lingering with you long after the curtain closes, hook the audience with compelling conflicts and resolutions. However, what makes this journey at times jarring are the interpretation and reaction to conflict of both Dragon and Creative.

The Dragon is the instigator, kicking up mud as she speeds through the office, searching for those who threaten her belonging. Her Shapeshifters monitor external threats—likely Creatives—whose excellence shakes the hierarchy, recalibrates the status quo, and charges them to call out unethical behavior. In resolution, the Dragon denigrates her victims, rewriting their scripts, making sure the last chapter concludes in their expulsion, assuring that their belonging to the community is permanently severed.

In contrast, the Creative shows up to work not to compete but for the love of the game. She is not one to instigate conflict, but often finds herself in one as she attempts to complete her work while trying to watch her back. For the Creative, the threat to belonging is internal; she reacts viscerally to the story scenes in which her values were violated, causing her to be thrown off her mission. In her search for healing, she must reconnect to her divine purpose and decide who and what she must abandon to fully inhabit her body, recommitting to belonging to herself and the larger big-tent community.

CONCLUSION

Workplace bullying can be seen as a complex quest for belonging, the Dragon meeting this need by creating a closed circle that amplifies her power and preserves her control by insisting on uniformity of thought. This notion of privileging one way of doing things is in direct contrast to the Creative's quest to erect a big tent that invites diverse perspectives and critical conversations, believing that innovation is spurred by free spaces that accommodate expansive wingspans where colleagues are trusted to take flight on their own paths, unencumbered by the risk of falling, believing that dips and diversions are essential to the larger journey.

The Creative's big tent, however, where everyone belongs, becomes the Dragon's kryptonite, threatening to infiltrate her closed circle of blind, committed followers.

Thus, in a desperate response to keep the closed circle from opening, the Dragon launches the bully war, in which the Creative's character is denigrated, coercing others to toss her out of the tent or risk their own expulsion. The fear of being othered, no longer belonging to oneself or the community, is so powerful that bystanders attempt to join the Dragon's closed circle, taking down the big tent of possibilities that nurtured their spirit.

Therefore, an organization's resolution to squelch bullying is fully dependent on crafting work cultures that eliminate closed circles and invite everyone under the big tent of belonging, celebrating diversity and infinite possibilities.

The chart below offers a quick recap of the theory of closed circles versus big-tent belonging.

Table 8.1. Theory of Closed Circles versus Big-Tent Belonging

	Construct	The Dragon	The Creative
Interpret	**Belief**	Scarcity	Abundance
	Values	Power and Compliance	Autonomy, Exploration, and Innovation
	Conflict	External	Internal
Strive for	**Goals**	Closed-Circle Belonging	Big-Tent Belonging

(continued)

Table 8.1 *(continued)*

	Construct	The Dragon	The Creative
Maintain	**Tools**	Humiliation and Belittlement, Gossip, Smear Campaign, Exclusion, Sabotage, Gaslighting, Ostracization, Retaliation	Intellectual Risk Taking, Deep Reflection, and Empathetic Care
	Setting as the Third Teacher	Strict Hierarchy, Homogeneous Thinking, Conflict Avoidant Communication, Lack of Constructive Feedback, Blame and Shame Response to Problems, and Failure of Figureheads to Protect the Creative	Flat Hierarchy, Autonomy, Cross-Collaboration, Problem Solving, and Encouragement to Take Intellectual Risks
	Working toward Resolution	Denigrate and Expel	Reconnect to Purpose and Decide Who or What to Give Up to Once Again Belong to Oneself

INVITATION #9

How do you define belonging, and what are the characters and characteristics of work cultures where you felt part of a community? Once the bullying began in earnest, how did it feel to be othered, cast out of the community? What steps did you take to rewrite your plotlines in a quest to belong once again to yourself?

Chapter 9

Concluding the Hero's Journey

A CLOSING LETTER

Dear Reader,

Here we are, starting this last chapter together, having journeyed through what first presented as a random road of abuse, only later to reveal itself as an intricate maze designed by the Dragon to be imposing and decentering, yet when looked at from an aerial view, contains a well-worn passageway.

So, the ruse is up. Though psychological terrorism on the job shakes the ground beneath the Creative's feet, causing shuddering disorientation, the cycle is actually quite predictable, making it possible for employees and organizations to develop a keen eye for identification and intervention, for that which can be predicted can be prevented, or at the very least, thoughtfully addressed and extinguished.

Along our walk together, we met some surly beasts and redemptive characters. First was the Creative, bold in thought and generous in spirit, whose ingenuity and free-thinking set off warning whistles for the keepers of the status quo. Next up was the Dragon and her complacent army of Shapeshifters, sometimes joined by the often delightful but highly malleable Community Builders. Finally, we pulled up an office chair to meet with some heads of organizations, a crapshoot of encounters. Are we sipping coffee with a Figurehead who enforces the hierarchy and paints the daily dealings opaque; or the Leader, a unicorn who crafts a transparent landscape, encouraging diverse collaborations while raising the ceiling so everyone's voice can rise?

With the characters identified in their natural habitat, we took a microscope to toxic settings where mold spurs regenerate, poisoning the air. We then examined the plotlines of workplace abuse, watching the six-part play, a predictable cycle of terrorism on the job.

Having built a foundation for understanding the characters and unfoldings, we explored the tools Dragons use to manipulate, sabotage, and exclude. We heard from the voices of victims about the fallout in the form of insidious emotional and physical suffering, ravaging the Creative's mind, body, and spirit, a war tactic that inflicts harm even after warriors leave the battleground and peace treaties are negotiated.

Despite the Creative's degradation, we learned of the redeeming opportunities nestled inside post-traumatic growth. As the journey reached its end, we looked at the hope embedded in creative cultures, reminding us to be loyal to our mission and purpose, a stance that at times demands that we seek new work when our current institution is clearly rotting.

Now, before we take off our work boots, readying to prop up our feet for a well-deserved rest, I follow this letter with a series of other creative tellings, leaving you with seeds of hope and pockets full of resources for your heart's mission as you carry out your purpose and search for unicorns.

Love, Dorothy

THE HELPING HANDS HELPLINES

Welcome to the evening show, *All Is Not Lost*. We begin tonight's episode with a segment on who to call when you need help. Be sure to applaud as locked doors open and you see the possibilities for soothing the skin where the Dragon burned you.

Remember, part of the Dragon's playbook is to isolate and shrink her victim, hoping he will vaporize, traceless, into the night. The following list is about scrapping scarcity thinking and dialing into the universe's abundance, recognizing that you are not alone, accepting the hands held out to help.

1. **National Workplace Bullying Coalition** aims to "Educate American workers and society in general about the existence of workplace bullying and the negative consequences of such a work culture that may inflict not only psychiatric injuries on the victim but also causes reduced productivity and increased medical and turnover expenditures for businesses." In addition, it works to:
   a. "Bring employers, employees, industry, non-profit groups, unions, legal representatives, workplace consultants, academic experts, organizational psychologists, community groups, and targets of abuse together to develop a bully-free work culture, including taking all necessary steps to prevent, detect, address, and remedy bullying in the workplace."
   b. "Work with legislatures at the local, state, and federal levels to refine the definition of workplace bullying and implement laws to protect workers' rights to dignity at work."[1]
2. **International Association on Workplace Bullying and Harassment** is the unifying, global professional organization for researchers and practitioners who study workplace bullying. The IAWBH includes members across thirty countries and holds a biannual international conference. The IAWBH is "is made up of scholars and practitioners who specialize in the field of workplace bullying and harassment." They "stimulate, generate, integrate and disseminate research and evidence-based practice in the field of workplace bullying and harassment."[2]
3. **Bergen Bullying Research Group** "is a research team at the University of Bergen in Norway devoted to research on workplace bullying and harassment, constructive and destructive forms of leadership, stress and emotions in organisations, and whistleblowing."[3]
4. **The Mobbing Portal** "aims to become a comprehensive guide to research literature on workplace mobbing, was begun in the Spring of 2008, as a project of the research team on academic mobbing at the University of Waterloo, Canada. The team is led by Kenneth Westhues, Professor of Sociology."[4]
5. **The Workplace Bullying Institute** "has focused on the prevention and correction of abusive conduct at work through

education of targets & the public, training of professionals, creation of evidence-based solutions for organizations and unions, research by WBI and others, and advocacy for a new law."[5]

6. **Minding The Workplace**; "this blog, hosted and written by David Yamada, is dedicated to news and commentary about work and employment relations. Dignity at work, workplace bullying, employment & labor law, and psychologically healthy work environments are recurring themes."[6]

7. **Dorothysuskind.com** is my personal website that includes research, articles, and an invitation to participate anonymously in workplace bullying studies.[7]

8. **Thrive-Wise Newsletter:** This is my weekly newsletter on Substack where I write articles and share resources on bullying in childhood and adolescents, workplace bullying, creativity, and how to build and sustain healthy families and work cultures.

9. **Psychology Today Blog: Bully-Wise: From Surviving to Thriving**. I am a regular contributor to *Psychology Today*, where each month I publish an article on a specific topic as it relates to workplace bullying.[8]

ADVICE I WISH SOMEONE HAD GIVEN ME

Each week, I have the opportunity to interview Creatives from around the world who have suffered the degradation of workplace abuse. As a narrative inquiry researcher, inside that conversation I rarely ask questions. In this sense, I am not interviewing at all, instead standing witness to another's pain, validating that her story is both real and devastating.

Inside that storytelling, many Creatives will share insights they stumbled upon on the battlefield, advice they wish they had received before the war started. Below, is a compendium of their reflections, an offering to others who are currently on the frontlines. Each suggestion provides strategies for protecting your emotional and physical health while reclaiming your power.

I am, of course, a researcher, not a lawyer or mental health professional, so these strategies should not be used as substitutes for seeking legal counsel or medical assistance. Now, let's learn from the Creatives.

- Before accepting a job, ask who served in your role prior, how long they were there for, and why they left. If a job has experienced high turnover, it may be a warning sign that a Dragon is in the house. It is often useful to talk to as many people as possible who previously worked at the organization. Don't rely solely on recommendations from employees who currently work there, for out of self-preservation, they may be reluctant to share the ugly truths. To deepen your search, explore various online sites where employees offer anonymous feedback on their experiences at the organization.
- Victims of workplace abuse suffer significant long-lasting trauma. In order to start the healing process, it is essential to find a therapist to assist you along the journey. Unfortunately, at times, therapists who are not trained in trauma-informed care and who do not understand the impact and cycle of workplace bullying, can unintentionally invalidate your experience, doing more harm than good. Make sure to interview numerous therapists to ensure the best fit, and don't be afraid to leave a therapist who is not meeting your needs.
- In addition to seeking therapy, join a support group for victims of workplace abuse. Within the United States, the National Workplace Bullying Coalition offers a variety of groups and resources to support victims of bullying.
- As soon as you discover you are being bullied, start to look for another job. Though at the time, leaving your employer may be difficult to fathom, it is important to know your options and start to devise a plan B. Simply creating an exit plan, even if you end up not needing it, will give you a sense of personal empowerment. Unfortunately, many Creatives resist entertaining the option of leaving until their health has deteriorated to such a degree that they are no longer in an emotional or physical state to engage in a job search.
- Keep a detailed account of each bullying incident. For each entry, record the date, time, description, and consequence. Avoid commentary; just stick to the facts.
- In addition to chronicling each bullying incident in writing, it is helpful to keep a journal. Throughout the day, when your

emotions are rising, take time to record your feelings. Such an exercise provides you a private outlet for expression. In addition, at a later date, if you start to question "if it is really all that bad," go back and read your earlier entries. As victims of workplace abuse, our feelings are often minimized and our experiences gaslighted; therefore, having a written record of your days can be incredibly useful and validating.

- A strategy for dealing with the Dragon or other abusive colleagues is to envision your body drifting to the ceiling, a passive observer looking down at the conversation. Then start an internal dialogue, speaking silently to yourself, where you name the behavior that the bully is engaging in. For example, you might say, "How very interesting—Dara is calling upon the invisible army, trying to make me feel like people are talking behind my back, when in reality, these are all manufactured lies. How sad that she is so insecure she has to resort to such tactics." This strategy helps you to separate from the abuse and name what is happening instead of being hooked emotionally by the situation.

- Remember that "no" is a complete sentence. You are not obligated to offer a detailed reasoning for your decision. For example, if the Dragon gives you a file folder at 4:40 p.m. on a Thursday afternoon and asks you to prepare a report by 8 a.m. the next day, simply say, "I appreciate you asking, but I am not able to finish this by the morning. I can, however, have it to you by Monday afternoon." If the Dragon insists that you work on a Saturday to host an event, clearly but politely answer, "Thank you for thinking of me, but I am not available to work on Saturday."

- In an effort to maintain your mental health, make it a practice to not open emails on Fridays after 3 p.m. Dragons often send emails intended to hook you emotionally at the end of the day and at the conclusion of the week, a tactic to keep you on guard and prevent you from healing outside of office hours.

- Many Creatives report having their personal items and files tampered with at work, a personal violation and a form of sabotage. Be careful not to leave any personal files or information at the office and make sure all work documents are locked and passcoded.

- If the Dragon calls your office or cell phone, do not take the call. If she can get you on the line and catch you off guard, she is more likely to cut you with her claws. Instead, let her leave a message, and call her back when you are adequately prepared emotionally. If she leaves a hostile message, make sure to save it as evidence. Upon your call back, at a time you determine, make sure to have your journal in front of you, so you can accurately capture the conversation in writing. It is also helpful to put the phone on speaker, if your state law allows it, so others can witness the abuse.
- If you are called to a meeting with the Dragon or Human Resources, insist on receiving an agenda beforehand. This will help you prepare and lessen the chance of being ambushed. If during the meeting other topics are brought up, politely say that you are not able to address that topic today as it was not on the agenda, but you are happy to revisit it during another scheduled time.
- If you show up at a meeting with the Dragon to discuss a specific topic stated on the agenda, and a representative from Human Resources is present, it is likely you are about to be ambushed. Consider stating that this is not the meeting you prepared for, so you will have to reschedule for another day. Ask them to send you a new date for the meeting including the agenda and the names of all people who will be present.
- During a planned meeting with a set agenda, if the Dragon begins to belittle you or make inflammatory statements, don't react emotionally. Instead, do one of two things. Option one is to say, "I am willing to discuss the issues at hand, but I must insist on a dignified exchange. If that is not possible at the moment, I will need to reschedule for another time." Option two is to say something like, "You know I like to keep a notebook as a record of all of my meetings and work agendas. I want to be sure to capture what you just said exactly. Could you please repeat that remark so I can record it verbatim?" Such a request will likely make the Dragon become more careful with her word choice and provide you with written documentation of the abuse that transpired.
- If you have an employment contract, make sure to print it and read it carefully. Often Dragons will make statements such as, "All employees are required to work on the weekends."

However, when Creatives carefully review their contract, they discover it clearly lays out the hours of eight to five on weekdays only.

- Before seeking help from upper management, investigate whether bullying is addressed in the company handbook. If so, print it and be prepared to use it as the foundation for seeking assistance.
- If you live in a country with protective work legislation, make sure you know the law. If you belong to a union, carefully understand your protections. Legal counsel can be invaluable in navigating these complex situations.
- If you decide to reach out to your boss's boss or Human Resources to report the bullying and seek support, understand that the likelihood is high that you will be retaliated against. It is also important to realize that chances are strong that your Dragon has already shared an unflattering narrative about you to her boss and Human Resources, so it is likely they have been primed to see you as the problem. This does not mean that you should not seek help; it just means that you should be prepared for the outcome. When sharing your bullying experience, resist using terms such as narcissist, psychopath, or bipolar. Instead, simply explain what happened and ask the person you are talking with to reflect on what you shared. Though these discussions will likely brew heated emotions inside of you, work hard to maintain your composure. It is helpful to write out what you want to say to give you an added source of support and prevent you from leaving out vital information.
- Make sure to nurture a true and compassionate circle of friends outside of work. One of the most devastating fallouts of being mobbed on the job is that colleagues you once considered dear friends and confidants will often begin to separate themselves from you out of fear of being targeted next. In addition, many eventually will join in on the attacks. When this happens, it is imperative to have true friends outside of your work circle who have your back, show you compassion, and would never consider leaving your side regardless of how choppy the waters.
- A number of Creatives in my study shared that their organizations deleted incriminating emails from their server to avoid

fallout or legal consequences. If your organization doesn't have policies against it, it is helpful to print emails that could be useful in documenting the abuse.

- Upon your departure, if you are offered a financial settlement in exchange for signing a nondisclosure agreement, seek the counsel of a lawyer. Never sign anything without giving it to a lawyer for review.
- If you seek legal counsel, it is tempting to go to the lowest bidder to save money. However, at times, hiring a seasoned employment lawyer, from a top firm, provides you more bargaining power and better equips you to work toward a more timely solution. Regardless, make sure that your legal team knows the research on workplace bullying and has a strong history of defending abuse victims.
- Remember who you are and make a commitment to yourself: regardless of what the Dragon does and how she acts, you will remain steadfast in your values.

GREETINGS WARRIOR

Greetings Warrior,

The final stage of the Hero's Journey, the monomyth, is upon us, where the hero—that's you—returns home with the elixir, stepping back to the beginning, but clothed anew, your former self no longer recognizable as you step onto this familiar yet foreign land.

It's a full-circle return. You are now completely encompassing your own skin, possessing a deeper understanding of self, a consequence of inner soul work.

Your identity now hangs on purpose and mission, no longer determined by the letters behind your name or title on your business cards. Today, you have a new message.

Seated at the table, pencil gripped, you redact the Dragon's rewrites, reclaiming your narrative, insisting that you are the only one who gets to tell your story.

Around your kitchen table, a group gathers. You see old faces, from this world before, ones who stood shoulder to shoulder, tall and bold, refusing to duck when your dignity was infiltrated. You see new faces, too, the ones you met in the hole you sank into, diverse and overlapping story lines providing a quiet corner where loneliness took a break for the evening as together you remembered how to breathe. Last, you see the future-tellers, seated at the end of the table, facing forward, the sun brushing the sides of their faces as they help you envision your tomorrow.

Congratulations! You have arrived home for the first time again.

Sincerely, Evolution

THERE WAS AN OLD WOMAN

An old woman refused to lay sidewalks over the field. Instead, she invited the children to run in their own directions, discovering paths that led to destinations that never appeared on the architect's blueprint. Oh, how she delighted in the children's excavations. Dragons do not understand that old woman. They think she was simply mad. When others inquire, "What if we did it this way instead?," they take their questions as a rebuke, beckon their minions to gossip, and call in the cavalry to block creativity. Their tactics are successful, and their room remains quite small. Look out the window at the woman walking new pathways, enlightenments only children and those who look at the world with infant eyes can walk and see.

REMEMBER

My heart still sleeps on the outside of my shirt. My imagination makes my skin glitter. My lights now glow in new rooms that expand across universes. Some days a tear disintegrates pieces of my healing. I still generously give away my heart. I am abundant. And you were, too.

DEAR DRAGONFLY

Dear Dragonfly,

Yesterday as I peered over the preschool fence, I watched you scale the top of the monkey bars instead of swinging from below. You said you liked the view, because it made you feel closer to the sun. The teacher hollered at you to get down before you got hurt, that it was dangerous, but you didn't budge, instead retorting, "But the boys do it all the time." I applaud your gusto and launch a prayer into the sky, "To keep breaking the rules, little Dragonfly." However, my heart worries that as you grow, they will paint a target on your superhero cape. Then, I remember that you are expansive, difficult to manipulate and control. Whacking aside my worries, I step to the pulpit, made of the rule books you discarded, and scream, "Keep scaling the tops of the monkey bars, supergirl," and then I bend down to pick up your little sister who wants to watch you fly.

Love, Mom

INVITATION #10

You can love yourself even when others don't love you. It is an empowering and radical reckoning that takes many of us far too many decades to stumble upon. Your capacity for self-compassion is not dependent on their measuring stick. You determine how tall you stand. Below, write a love letter to yourself, proclaiming your complete devotion to the sacredness of your soul. You do not need to earn your worthiness; that gift was bestowed in perpetuity at your creation.

Be gentle with yourself as you prepare to fly again.

This concludes our journey, fellow Creatives. I hope you will keep in touch. Walk boldly, think expansively, and look out for unicorns; better yet, become one.

Notes

PRELUDE

1. "Workplace Bullying," National Workplace Bullying Coalition, August 1, 2022, https://www.workplacebullyingcoalition.org.
2. Elisabeth Kübler-Ross, *On Death and Dying* (New York: Collier Books, 1993).
3. Joseph Campbell, *The Hero with a Thousand Faces*, 2nd ed. (Princeton, NJ: Princeton University Press, 1972).

INTRODUCTION

1. F. Michael Connelly and D. Jean Clandinin, "Stories of Experience and Narrative Inquiry," *Educational Researcher* 19, no. 5 (1990): 2.
2. D. Jean Clandinin, M. Shaun Murphy, Janice Huber, and Anne Murray Orr, "Negotiating Narrative Inquiries: Living in a Tension-Filled Midst," *Journal of Educational Research* 103, no. 2 (2010): 81–90.
3. Ben Okri, *A Way of Being Free* (London: Head of Zeus, 2014), 46.
4. Ian Beech, "Bracketing in Phenomenological Research," *Nurse Researcher* 6, no. 3 (1999): 35–51.
5. John W. Creswell, *Qualitative Inquiry and Research Design: Choosing among Five Approaches*, 3rd ed. (London: Sage, 2013).
6. Helene Starks and Susan Brown Trinidad, "Choose Your Method: A Comparison of Phenomenology, Discourse Analysis, and Grounded Theory," *Qualitative Health Research* 17, no. 10 (2007): 1372–80.
7. Carolyn Ellis, Tony E. Adams, and Arthur P. Bochner, "Autoethnography: An Overview," *Historical Social Research/Historische Sozialforschung* 36, no. 4 (2011): 273–90.

8. Ronald Pelias, *A Poetics of Personal Relations* (Walnut Creek, CA: Left Coast Press, 2011), 12.

9. Thomas (Tom) E. Barone and Elliot W. W. Eisner, *Arts Based Research* (Thousand Oaks, CA: Sage, 2011), 8–9.

10. Dorothy Suskind, "Bully-Wise: From Surviving to Thriving," *Psychology Today*, https://www.psychologytoday.com/us/blog/bully-wise, accessed July 28, 2022.

11. G. Namie and R. Namie, *The Bully-Free Workplace: Stop Jerks, Weasels, and Snakes from Killing Your Organization* (New York: Wiley, 2011).

12. D. Hampton, K. Tharp-Barrie, and M. Kay Rayens, "Experience of Nursing Leaders with Workplace Bullying and How to Best Cope," *Journal of Nursing Management* 27, no. 3 (2019): 517–26, https://doi.org/10.1111/jonm.12706; Premilla D'Cruz, Ernesto Noronha, and Pamela Lutgen-Sandvik, "Power, Subjectivity and Context in Workplace Bullying, Emotional Abuse and Harassment: Insights from Postpositivism," *Qualitative Research in Organizations and Management: An International Journal* 13, no. 1 (Bradford, West Yorkshire: Emerald Publishing, 2018), https://public.ebookcentral.proquest.com/choice/publicfullrecord.aspx?p=5351433; Darla J. Twale, *Understanding and Preventing Faculty-On-Faculty Bullying: A Psycho-Social-Organizational Approach* (New York: Routledge, 2018).

CHAPTER 1

1. Joseph Campbell, *The Hero with a Thousand Faces*, 2nd ed. (Princeton, NJ: Princeton University Press, 1972).

CHAPTER 2

1. Snejina Michailova and Kenneth Husted, "Knowledge-Sharing Hostility in Russian Firms," *California Management Review* 45, no. 3 (2003): 59–77.

2. Shilpee Dasgupta, Damodar Suar, and Seema Singh, "Managerial Communication Practices and Employees' Attitudes and Behaviors," *Corporate Communications: An International Journal* 19, no. 3 (2014): 287–302; Gongmin Bao, Bixiang Xu, and Zhongyuan Zhang, "Employees' Trust and Their Knowledge Sharing and Integration: The Mediating Roles of Organizational Identification and Organization-Based Self-Esteem," *Knowledge Management Research & Practice* 14, no. 3 (2016): 362–75.

3. Maria Konnikova, "Messy: The Power of Disorder to Transform Our Lives by Tim Harford," *New York Times Book Review* 121, no. 42 (2016): 21.

4. Younyoung Choi, "The Influence of Conflict Management Culture on Job Satisfaction," *Social Behavior and Personality: An International Journal* 41, no. 4 (2013): 687–92.

5. Janice K. Kiecolt-Glaser, "Marriage, Divorce, and the Immune System," *American Psychologist* 73, no. 9 (2018): 1098–1108.

6. Kerry Patterson, *Crucial Conversation: Tools for Talking When Stakes Are High* (New York: McGraw-Hill, 2002).

7. Shelly J. Cornell and Caroline Simard, "Research: Vague Feedback Is Holding Women Back," *Harvard Business Review*, April 29, 2016.

8. Liz Fosslien and Mollie West Duffy, *No Hard Feelings: The Secret Power of Embracing Emotions at Work* (New York: Portfolio, 2019).

9. Ira Levin, *The Stepford Wives* (New York: Random House, 1972).

10. John McClure and James Brown, "Belonging at Work," *Human Resource Development International* 11, no. 1 (2008): 3–17.

11. Julie Rozovsky, "The Five Keys to a Successful Google Team," *re:Work*, November 17, 2015, https://rework.withgoogle.com/blog/five-keys-to-a-successful-google-team/.

12. Amy Edmondson, *The Fearless Organization: Creating Psychological Safety in the Workplace for Learning, Innovation, and Growth* (Hoboken, NJ: Wiley, 2019).

13. Alfie Kohn, "Digging Themselves in Deeper: More Misleading Claims about the Value of Homework," *Phi Delta Kappan* 88, no. 7 (2007): 514–17.

14. Mariam Orkodashvili, "Corruption, Collusion, and Nepotism in Higher Education and the Labor Market in Georgia," *European Education* 43, no. 2 (2011): 32–53.

15. Adam Below, *In Praise of Nepotism: A Natural History* (New York: Doubleday, 2003); Margaret Y. Padgett, Robert J. Padgett, and Kathryn A. Morris, "Perceptions of Nepotism Beneficiaries: The Hidden Price of Using a Family Connection to Obtain a Job," *Journal of Business and Psychology* 30, no. 2 (2015): 283–98.

16. Ronnie Janoff-Bulman, *Shattered Assumptions: Towards a New Psychology of Trauma* (New York: Simon & Schuster, 2010).

17. Janet P. Near and Marcia P Miceli, "Organizational Dissidence: The Case of Whistle-Blowing," *Journal of Business Ethics* 4, no. 1 (1985): 1–16.

18. McKenzie R. Rees, Ann E. Tenbrunsel, and Max H. Bazerman, "Bounded Ethicality and Ethical Fading in Negotiations: Understanding Unintended Unethical Behavior," *Academy of Management Perspectives* 33, no. 1 (2019): 26–42; Jessica R. Mesmer-Magnus and Chockalingam Viswesvaran, "Whistleblowing in Organizations: An Examination of Correlates of Whistleblowing Intentions, Actions, and Retaliation," *Journal of Business Ethics* 62, no. 3 (2005): 277–97.

19. John Solas, "Conscientious Objections to Corporate Wrongdoing," *Business and Society Review* 124, no. 1 (2019): 43–62, https://doi.org/10.1111/basr.12162.

20. Luciano Floridi, "Faultless Responsibility: On the Nature and Allocation of Moral Responsibility for Distributed Moral Actions," *Philosophical Transactions: Mathematical, Physical and Engineering Sciences* 374, no. 2083 (2016): 1–13.

21. Tom Devine, Tarek F. Maassarani, and Government Accountability Project, *The Corporate Whistleblower's Survival Guide: A Handbook for Committing the Truth* (San Francisco: Berrett-Koehler, 2011).

22. Delroy L. Paulhus and Kevin M. Williams, "The Dark Triad of Personality: Narcissism, Machiavellianism, and Psychopathy," *Journal of Research in Personality* 36, no. 6 (2002): 556–63.

CHAPTER 3

1. Joseph Campbell, *The Hero with a Thousand Faces*, 2nd ed. (Princeton, NJ: Princeton University Press, 1972).

2. J. K. Rowling, *Harry Potter and the Sorcerer's Stone* (New York: Scholastic Press, 1998); *Star Wars*, Lucasfilm, 2000.

3. Heinz Leymann, "Mobbing and Psychological Terror at Workplaces," *Violence and Victims* 5, no. 2 (1990): 11–126; Maureen P. Duffy and Len Sperry, *Mobbing: Causes, Consequences, and Solutions* (Oxford, UK: Oxford University Press, 2012); Noa Davenport, Ruth Distler Schwartz, and Gail Pursell Elliott, *Mobbing: Emotional Abuse in the American Workplace* (Ames, IA: Civil Society, 2005).

4. Gary Namie, *U.S. Workplace Bullying Survey*, Workplace Bullying Institute, Zogby Analytics (pollster), 2021.

CHAPTER 4

1. Jerry A. Carbo, *Understanding, Defining and Eliminating Workplace Bullying: Assuring Dignity at Work* (Abingdon, Oxon: Routledge, 2017); Einarsen Ståle, Helge Hoel, Dieter Zapf, and Cary L. Cooper, eds., *Bullying and Harassment in the Workplace: Theory, Research and Practice*, 3rd ed. (Abingdon, Oxon: Routledge, 2020).

2. Laura Cox Dzurec, "Examining 'Sticky' Storytelling and Moral Claims as the Essence of Workplace Bullying," *Nursing Outlook* 68, no. 5 (2020): 647–56.

3. Brené Brown, *Braving the Wilderness: The Quest for True Belonging and the Courage to Stand Alone* (New York: Random House, 2019).

4. Patrick Hamilton, *Gas Light: A Victorian Thriller in Three Acts* (London: Constable, 1939).

5. Leslie Ann Locke and Sonya D. Hayes, "Navigating the Gendered Labyrinths and Managing the Mean Girls and Queen Bees within the Academy: A Dialogue between Two Women Assistant Professors," *Sojo Journal: Educational Foundations and Social Justice Education* 6, nos. 1–2 (2020): 41–55; Deborah Philips, "Gaslighting: Domestic Noir, the Narratives of Coercive Control," *Women: A Cultural Review* 32, no. 2 (2021): 140–60.

6. Dominic Abrams, Michael A. Hogg, and José M. Marques, *The Social Psychology of Inclusion and Exclusion* (New York: Psychology Press, 2005).

7. Kipling D. Williams and Lisa Zadro, "Interpersonal Rejection," in *Ostracism: On Being Ignored, Excluded, and Rejected* (Oxford, UK: Oxford University Press, 2006); Y. Mao, C. Jiang, Y. Liu, and I. D. Zhang, "Why Am I Ostracized and How Would I React? A Review of Workplace Ostracism Research," *Asia Pacific Journal of Management* 35, no. 3 (2018): 745–67.

8. L. Frank Baum, *The Wonderful Wizard of Oz* (Minneapolis, MN: Lerner, 2014).

9. Dana Morningstar, *Out of the Fog: Moving from Confusion to Clarity after Narcissistic Abuse* (Mason, MI: Morningstar Media, 2018).

CHAPTER 5

1. Harold Garfinkel, "Conditions of Successful Degradation Ceremonies," *American Journal of Sociology* 61, no. 5 (1956): 420–24; Erving Goffman, *Stigma: Notes on the Management of Spoiled Identity* (New York: Simon & Schuster, 1963).

2. Goffman, *Stigma*.

3. Garfinkel, "Conditions of Successful Degradation Ceremonies."

4. Ken Jennings, "The Origin of the Phrase 'Beyond the Pale,'" October 10, 2016, https://www.cntraveler.com/story/what-beyond-the-pale-actually.

5. Paul Maurice Conway, Thomas Clausen, Åse Marie Hansen, and Annie Hogh, "Workplace Bullying and Sickness Presenteeism: Cross-Sectional and Prospective Associations in a 2-Year Follow-Up Study," *International Archives of Occupational and Environmental Health* 89, no. 1 (2016): 103–14.

6. Ronnie Janoff-Bulman, *Shattered Assumptions: Towards a New Psychology of Trauma* (New York: Simon & Schuster, 2010).

7. Janoff-Bulman, *Shattered Assumptions*; Mieneke Pouwelse, Roelie Mulder, Eva Gemzøe Mikkelsen, P. D'Cruz, E. Noronha, E. Baillien, B. Catley, K. Harlos, A. Hogh, and E. Gemzøe Mikkelsen, "Pathways of Job-Related Negative Behavior: Handbooks of Workplace Bullying, Emotional Abuse and Harassment," 2, 1–37, in *The Role of Bystanders in Workplace Bullying: An Overview of Theories and Empirical Research* (Singapore: Springer, 2019), 6–27.

8. Kirsten Nabe-Nielsen, Matias Brødsgaard Grynderup, Theis Lange, Johan Hviid Andersen, Jens Peter Bonde, Paul Maurice Conway, Anne

Helene Garde, et al., "The Role of Poor Sleep in the Relation between Workplace Bullying/Unwanted Sexual Attention and Long-Term Sickness Absence," *International Archives of Occupational and Environmental Health* 89, no. 6 (2016): 967–79.

9. Martial Berset, Norbert Semmer, Achim Elfering, Nicola Jacobshagen, and Laurenz Meier, "Does Stress at Work Make You Gain Weight? A Two-Year Longitudinal Study," *Scandinavian Journal of Work, Environment & Health*, 37 no. 1 (2011): 45–53.

10. Isabel Lever, Daniel Dyball, Neil Greenberg, and Sharon A. M. Stevelink, "Health Consequences of Bullying in the Healthcare Workplace: A Systematic Review," *Journal of Advanced Nursing* 75, no. 12 (2019): 3195–3209.

11. Christopher Magee, Ross Gordon, Laura Robinson, Peter Caputi, and Lindsay Oades, "Workplace Bullying and Absenteeism: The Mediating Roles of Poor Health and Work Engagement," *Human Resource Management Journal* 27, no. 3 (2017): 319–34; Heidi Janssens, Lutgart Braeckman, Bart De Clercq, Annalisa Casini, Dirk De Bacquer, France Kittel, and Els Clays, "The Indirect Association of Job Strain with Long-Term Sickness Absence through Bullying: A Mediation Analysis Using Structural Equation Modeling," *BMC Public Health* 16, no. 1 (2016): 851–51; B. Verkuil, S. Atasayi, and M. L. Molendijk, "Workplace Bullying and Mental Health: A Meta-Analysis on Cross-Sectional and Longitudinal Data," *PLoS One* 10, no. 8 (2015), https://doi.org/1156 10.1371/journal.pone.0135225; Conway, Clausen, Hansen, and Hogh, "Workplace Bullying and Sickness Presenteeism."

12. Duncan Lewis, "Bullying at Work: The Impact of Shame among University and College Lecturers," *British Journal of Guidance & Counselling* 32, no. 3 (2004): 281–99; Lillemor R. M. Hallberg and Margaretha K. Strandmark, "Health Consequences of Workplace Bullying: Experiences from the Perspective of Employees in the Public Service Sector," *International Journal of Qualitative Research* 1, no. 2 (2006): 109–19.

13. Helge Hoel, Charlotte Rayner, and Cary Cooper, "Workplace Bullying," *International Review of Industrial Organizational Psychology*, 14 (1999): 195–229.

14. Alessandro Lo Presti, Paolo Pappone, and Alfonso Landolfi, "The Associations between Workplace Bullying and Physical or Psychological Negative Symptoms: Anxiety and Depression as Mediators," *Europe's Journal of Psychology* 15, no. 4 (2019): 808–22.

15. Lewis, "Bullying at Work"; Tara Gruenewald, Margaret Kemeny, Najib Aziz, and John Fahey, "Acute Threat to the Social Self: Shame, Social Self-Esteem, and Cortisol Activity," *Psychosomatic Medicine*, 66 (2004): 915–24.

16. Åse Marie Hansen, *Workplace Bullying, Stress Response and Long-Term Sickness Absence-Exploring Mechanisms: Results from Six Cohort Studies* (Copenhagen: Faculty of Health and Medical Sciences, University of Copenhagen).

17. Zeynep Baran Tatar and Yüksel Şahika, "Mobbing at Workplace: Psychological Trauma and Documentation of Psychiatric Symptoms," *Archives of Neuropsychiatry* 56, no. 1 (2019): 57–62; Morten Birkeland Nielsen, Marianne Skogbrott Birkeland, Marianne Bang Hansen, Stein Knardahl, and Trond Heir, "Victimization from Workplace Bullying after a Traumatic Event: Time-Lagged Relationships with Symptoms of Posttraumatic Stress," *International Archives of Occupational and Environmental Health* 90, no. 5 (2017): 411–21.

18. Kipling D. Williams and Lisa Zadro, "Interpersonal Rejection," in *Ostracism: On Being Ignored, Excluded, and Rejected* (Oxford, UK: Oxford University Press, 2006).

19. Eric Jones and Janice Kelly, "'Why Am I Out of the Loop?' Attributions Influence Responses to Information Exclusion," *Personality and Social Psychology Bulletin* 36, no. 9 (2010): 1186–1201.

20. Y. Mao, C. Jiang, Y. Liu, and I. D. Zhang, "Why Am I Ostracized and How Would I React? A Review of Workplace Ostracism Research," *Asia Pacific Journal of Management* 35, no. 3 (2018): 745–67.

21. Myriam Tong, Rene Schwendimann, and Franziska Zúñiga, "Mobbing among Care Workers in Nursing Homes: A Cross-Sectional Secondary Analysis of the Swiss Nursing Homes Human Resources Project," *International Journal of Nursing Studies*, 66 (2017): 72–81.

22. Michael Rosander, Denise Salin, and Stefan Blomberg, "The Last Resort: Workplace Bullying and the Consequences of Changing Jobs," *Scandinavian Journal of Psychology* 63, no. 2 (2022): 124–35.

23. Conway, Clausen, Hansen, and Hogh, "Workplace Bullying and Sickness Presenteeism."

24. Catalina Sau Man Ng, "Effects of Workplace Bullying on Chinese Children's Health, Behaviours and School Adjustment Via Parenting: Study Protocol for a Longitudinal Study," *BMC Public Health* 19, no. 1 (2019): 1–12.

25. Naima Akhtar Malik and Kaj Björkqvist, "Workplace Bullying and Occupational Stress among University Teachers: Mediating and Moderating Factors," *Europe's Journal of Psychology*, 2 (2019): 240–59.

26. Liana S. Leach, Carmel Poyser, and Peter Butterworth, "Workplace Bullying and the Association with Suicidal Ideation/Thoughts and Behaviour: A Systematic Review," *Occupational and Environmental Medicine* 74, no. 1 (2017): 72–79.

27. Morten Birkeland Nielsen, Geir Høstmark Nielsen, Guy Notelaers, and Ståle Einarsen, "Workplace Bullying and Suicidal Ideation: A 3-Wave Longitudinal Norwegian Study," *American Journal of Public Health* 105, no. 11 (2015): 23–28.

CHAPTER 6

1. David Kessler, *Finding Meaning: The Sixth Stage of Grief* (New York: Scribner, 2020), 29.

2. Kessler, *Finding Meaning*.

3. Harold S. Kushner, *When Bad Things Happen to Good People* (New York: Schocken, 1981), 161.

4. Richard G. Tedeschi and Lawrence G. Calhoun, "Posttraumatic Growth: Conceptual Foundations and Empirical Evidence," *Psychological Inquiry* 15, no. 1 (2004): 1–18.

5. Richard G. Tedeschi and Lawrence G. Calhoun, "The Posttraumatic Growth Inventory: Measuring the Positive Legacy of Trauma," *Journal of Traumatic Stress* 9, no. 3 (1996): 455–71.

6. Richard G. Tedeschi, *Posttraumatic Growth: Theory, Research and Applications* (New York, Routledge, 2018).

7. Friedrich Wilhelm Nietzsche, *Twilight of the Idols*, Dover Thrift Editions (Mineola, NY: Dover, 2019), 6.

8. Ronnie Janoff-Bulman, *Shattered Assumptions: Towards a New Psychology of Trauma* (New York: Simon & Schuster, 2010).

9. Stephen Joseph, *What Doesn't Kill Us: The New Psychology of Posttraumatic Growth* (New York: Basic Books, 2011).

10. Candice Kumai, *Kintsugi Wellness: The Japanese Art of Nourishing Mind, Body, and Soul* (New York: HarperCollins, 2018).

11. Dorothy Suskind, "Writing: An Act of Revolution," *English Journal* 111, no. 4 (2022): 17–19.

12. Tedeschi and Calhoun, "The Posttraumatic Growth Inventory."

13. James Pennebaker, "The Effects of Traumatic Disclosure on Physical and Mental Health: The Values of Writing and Talking about Upsetting Events," *International Journal of Emergency Mental Health* 1, no. 1 (1999): 9–18.

14. Viktor E. Frankl, *Man's Search for Meaning: An Introduction to Logotherapy*, 4th ed. (Cutchogue, NY: Buccaneer Books, 1992).

15. Michael White, *Narrative Practice: Continuing the Conversation* (New York: Norton, 2011).

16. Alice Morgan, *What Is Narrative Therapy? An Easy-to-Read Introduction* (Adelaide, South Australia: Dulwich Centre Publication, 2000).

17. White, *Narrative Practice*, 125.

18. David Denborough, *Retelling the Stories of Our Lives: Everyday Narrative Therapy to Draw Inspiration and Transform Experience* (New York: Norton, 2014).

19. James Pennebaker and John Evans, *Expressive Writing: Words That Heal* (Enumclaw, WA: Idyll Arbor, 2014).

20. White, *Narrative Practice*; Pennebaker and Evans, *Expressive Writing*; Denborough, *Retelling the Stories of Our Lives*.

21. Charlie Anders, *Never Say You Can't Survive: How to Get Through the Hard Times by Making Up Stories* (New York: St. Martin's, 2021), 73.

22. Mario E. Martinez, *The Mindbody Code: How to Change the Beliefs That Limit Your Health, Longevity, and Success* (Boulder, CO: Sounds True, 2016); Mario E. Martinez, *The Mindbody Self: How Longevity Is Culturally Learned and the Causes of Health Are Inherited* (Carlsbad, CA: Hay House, 2017).

CHAPTER 7

1. Michael De Luca, Rachael Horovitz, Brad Pitt, Scott Rudin, Andrew Karsch, Sidney Kimmel, Mark Bakshi, et al., *Moneyball* (Culver City, CA: Sony Pictures Home Entertainment, 2012).

2. David N. Perkins, *The Mind's Best Work* (Cambridge, MA: Harvard University Press, 1981).

3. Donald Murray, "The Maker's Eye," in B. Ballenger, ed., *The Curious Writer* (New York: Pearson, 2004), 421–25.

4. Mihaly Csikszentmihalyi, *Creativity: Flow and the Psychology of Discovery and Invention* (New York: HarperPerennial, 1997), 73.

5. David J. Epstein, *Range: Why Generalists Triumph in a Specialized World* (New York: Riverhead Books, 2021).

6. Yi Grace Ji and Cheng Hong, "Engaging Employees in CEO Activism: The Role of Transparent Leadership Communication in Making a Social Impact," *Journalism & Mass Communication Quarterly*, 2022.

7. Tae-Yeol Kim, Jie Wang, and Junsong Chen, "Mutual Trust between Leader and Subordinate and Employee Outcomes," *Journal of Business Ethics* 149, no. 4 (2018): 945–58.

8. Arie Sherman and Tal Shavit, "The Thrill of Creative Effort at Work: An Empirical Study on Work, Creative Effort and Well-Being," *Journal of Happiness Studies: An Interdisciplinary Forum on Subjective Well-Being* 19, no. 7 (2018): 2049–69.

9. Kerry Patterson, *Crucial Conversation: Tools for Talking When Stakes Are High* (New York: McGraw-Hill, 2002).

10. Kate Kenny, *Whistleblowing: Toward a New Theory* (Cambridge, MA: Harvard University Press, 2019).

11. Martin E. P. Seligman and Mihaly Csikszentmihalyi, "Positive Psychology: An Introduction," *American Psychologist* 55, no. 1 (2000): 5–14.

12. Maria Christina Meyers, Byron G. Adams, Lusanda Sekaja, Carmen Buzea, Ana-Maria Cazan, Mihaela Gotea, Delia Stefenel, and Marianne van Woerkom, "Perceived Organizational Support for the Use of Employees' Strengths and Employee Well-Being: A Cross-Country Comparison," *Journal of Happiness Studies: An Interdisciplinary Forum on Subjective Well-Being* 20, no. 6 (2019): 1825–41.

13. Inga Hoever, J. Zhou, and Daan Knippenberg, "Different Strokes for Different Teams: The Contingent Effects of Positive and Negative Feedback on the Creativity of Informationally Homogeneous and Diverse Teams," *Academy of Management Journal* 61, no. 6 (2017): 2159–81.

14. Jakob Mainert, Christoph Niepel, Kevin R. Murphy, and Samuel Greiff, "The Incremental Contribution of Complex Problem-Solving Skills to the Prediction of Job Level, Job Complexity, and Salary," *Journal of Business and Psychology* 34, no. 6 (2019): 825–45; Ishani Aggarwal and Anita Williams Woolley, "Team Creativity, Cognition, and Cognitive Style Diversity," *Management Science* 65, no. 4 (2019): 1586–99.

15. Susana Nascimento and Pólvora Alexandre, "Maker Cultures and the Prospects for Technological Action," *Science and Engineering Ethics* 24, no. 3 (2018): 927–46, https://doi.org/10.1007/s11948-016-9796-8.

16. Fatimah Lateef, "Maximizing Learning and Creativity: Understanding Psychological Safety in Simulation-Based Learning," *Journal of Emergencies, Trauma, and Shock* 13, no. 1 (2020): 5–14; Jia Hu, Berrin Erdogan, Kaifeng Jiang, Talya N. Bauer, and Songbo Liu, "Leader Humility and Team Creativity: The Role of Team Information Sharing, Psychological Safety, and Power Distance," *Journal of Applied Psychology* 103, no. 3 (2018): 313–23.

17. Magnus Hontvedt, Kenneth Silseth, and Line Wittek, "Professional Collaboration in Teacher Support Teams—A Study of Teacher and Nurse Educators' Creative Problem-Solving in a Shared Space for Professional Development," *Scandinavian Journal of Educational Research* 65, no. 2 (2021): 240–57; Wendy Moffat, "Creativity and Collaboration in the Small College Department," *Pedagogy* 10, no. 2 (2010): 283–94.

18. Lee Ann Waltz, Laura Muñoz, Holly Weber Johnson, and Tracy Rodriguez, "Exploring Job Satisfaction and Workplace Engagement in Millennial Nurses," *Journal of Nursing Management* 28, no. 3 (2020): 673–81.

19. Ercole Albertini and David P. J. Smith, "A Spiritual Audit of a Retail Branch of South African Bank: Original Research," *SA Journal of Human Resource Management* 6, no. 1 (2008): 10–21; Jie Feng, Yucheng Zhang, Xinmei Liu, Long Zhang, and Xiao Han, "Just the Right Amount of Ethics Inspires Creativity: A Cross-Level Investigation of Ethical Leadership, Intrinsic Motivation, and Employee Creativity," *Journal of Business Ethics*, 153 (2018): 645–58.

CHAPTER 8

1. Ståle Einarsen, Helge Hoel, Dieter Zapf, and Cary L. Cooper, eds., *Bullying and Harassment in the Workplace: Theory, Research and Practice*, 3rd ed. (Abingdon, Oxon: Routledge, 2020).

2. Konrad Lorenz, *Aggression: Background and Nature* (Stockholm: Norstedt & Söner, 1966).

3. Heinz Leymann, "Mobbing and Psychological Terror at Workplaces," *Violence and Victims* 5, no. 2 (1990): 119–26.

4. Ståle Einarsen, "The Nature and Causes of Bullying," *International Journal of Manpower*, 20 (1999): 16–27.

5. Ken Westhues, *The Envy of Excellence: Administrative Mobbing of High-Achieving Professors* (Lewiston, NY: Tribunal for Academic Justice/Edwin Mellen Press, 2005).

6. Noa Davenport, Ruth Schwartz, and Gail Elliott, *Mobbing: Emotional Abuse in the American Workplace* (Ames, IA: Civil Society, 2005); "The Workplace Bullying Institute." https://workplacebullying.org, accessed August 1, 2022.

7. "National Workplace Bullying Coalition," August 1, 2022, https://www.workplacebullyingcoalition.org.

8. Maureen P. Duffy and Len Sperry, *Mobbing: Causes, Consequences, and Solutions* (Oxford: Oxford University Press, 2012); Maureen Duffy and Len Sperry, *Overcoming Mobbing: A Recovery Guide for Workplace Aggression and Bullying* (Oxford: Oxford University Press, 2013).

9. Robert Hare, *Without Conscience: The Disturbing World of the Psychopaths among Us* (New York: Pocket Books, 1993).

10. Paul Babiak and Robert D. Hare, *Snakes in Suits: When Psychopaths Go to Work* (New York: Regan Books, 2006).

11. Carolyn Pope, Lella Gandini Edwards, and George E. Forman, *The Hundred Languages of Children: The Reggio Emilia Experience in Transformation* (Santa Barbara, CA: Praeger, 2012).

CHAPTER 9

1. National Workplace Bullying Coalition, "About," https://www.workplacebullyingcoalition.org, accessed July 28, 2022.

2. International Association on Workplace Bullying and Harassment, "Home," https://www.iawbh.org, accessed July 28, 2022.

3. The Bergman Bullying Research Group, "About," https://www.uib.no/en/rg/bbrg, accessed August 6, 2022.

4. The Mobbing Portal, "About Us," http://www.mobbingportal.com/aboutus.html, accessed August 6, 2022.

5. Workplace Bullying Institute, https://workplacebullying.org, accessed August 6, 2022.

6. Minding Your Mind at Work, "About This Blog and NWI," https://newworkplace.wordpress.com/about/, accessed August 6, 2022.

7. Dorothy Suskind, Bully-Wise, "Dear Reader," https://www.bully-wise
.com, accessed August 6, 2022.

8. Dorothy Suskind, "Bully-Wise: From Surviving to Thriving," https://
www.psychologytoday.com/us/blog/bully-wise, accessed July 28, 2022.

Bibliography

Abrams, Dominic, Michael A. Hogg, and José M. Marques. *The Social Psychology of Inclusion and Exclusion*. New York: Psychology Press, 2005.

Aggarwal, Ishani, and Anita Williams Woolley. "Team Creativity, Cognition, and Cognitive Style Diversity." *Management Science* 65, no. 4 (2019): 1586–99.

Albertini, Ercole, and David P. J. Smith. "A Spiritual Audit of a Retail Branch of South African Bank: Original Research." *SA Journal of Human Resource Management* 6, no. 1 (2008): 10–21.

Anders, Charlie. *Never Say You Can't Survive: How to Get Through the Hard Times by Making Up Stories*. New York: St. Martin's Press, 2021.

Babiak, Paul, and Robert D. Hare. *Snakes in Suits: When Psychopaths Go to Work*. New York: Regan Books, 2006.

Bao, Gongmin, Bixiang Xu, and Zhongyuan Zhang. "Employees' Trust and Their Knowledge Sharing and Integration: The Mediating Roles of Organizational Identification and Organization-Based Self-Esteem." *Knowledge Management Research & Practice* 14, no. 3 (2016): 362–75.

Barone, Thomas E., and Elliot W. W. Eisner. *Arts Based Research*. Thousand Oaks, CA: Sage, 2011.

Baum, L. Frank. *The Wonderful Wizard of Oz*. Minneapolis, MN: Lerner, 2014.

Beech, Ian. "Bracketing in Phenomenological Research." *Nurse Researcher* 6, no. 3 (1999): 35–51.

Below, Adam. *In Praise of Nepotism: A Natural History*. New York: Doubleday, 2003.

Berset, Martial, Norbert Semmer, Achim Elfering, Nicola Jacobshagen, and Laurenz Meier. "Does Stress at Work Make You Gain Weight? A Two-Year Longitudinal Study." *Scandinavian Journal of Work, Environment & Health*, 37, no. 1 (2011): 45–53.

Brown, Brené. *Braving the Wilderness: The Quest for True Belonging and the Courage to Stand Alone*. New York: Random House, 2019.

Campbell, Joseph. *The Hero with a Thousand Faces*, 2nd ed. Princeton, NJ: Princeton University Press, 1972.

Carbo, Jerry A. *Understanding, Defining and Eliminating Workplace Bullying: Assuring Dignity at Work*. Abingdon, Oxon: Routledge, 2017.

Choi, Younyoung. "The Influence of Conflict Management Culture on Job Satisfaction." *Social Behavior and Personality: An International Journal* 41, no. 4 (2013): 687–92.

Clandinin, D. Jean, M. Shaun Murphy, Janice Huber, and Anne Murray Orr. "Negotiating Narrative Inquiries: Living in a Tension-Filled Midst." *Journal of Educational Research* 103, no. 2 (2010): 81–90.

Connelly, F. Michael, and D. Jean Clandinin. "Stories of Experience and Narrative Inquiry." *Educational Researcher* 19, no. 5 (1990): 2.

Conway, Paul Maurice, Thomas Clausen, Åse Marie Hansen, and Annie Hogh. "Workplace Bullying and Sickness Presenteeism: Cross-Sectional and Prospective Associations in a 2-Year Follow-Up Study." *International Archives of Occupational and Environmental Health* 89, no. 1 (2016): 103–14.

Cornell, Shelly J., and Caroline Simard. "Research: Vague Feedback Is Holding Women Back." *Harvard Business Review*, April 29, 2016.

Creswell, John W. *Qualitative Inquiry and Research Design: Choosing among Five Approaches*, 3rd ed. London: Sage, 2013.

Csikszentmihalyi, Mihaly. *Creativity: Flow and the Psychology of Discovery and Invention*. New York: HarperPerennial, 1997.

Dasgupta, Shilpee, Damodar Suar, and Seema Singh. "Managerial Communication Practices and Employees' Attitudes and Behaviors." *Corporate Communications: An International Journal* 19, no. 3 (2014): 287–302.

Davenport, Noa, Ruth Distler Schwartz, and Gail Pursell Elliott. *Mobbing: Emotional Abuse in the American Workplace*. Ames, IA: Civil Society, 2005.

D'Cruz, Premilla, Ernesto Noronha, and Pamela Lutgen-Sandvik. "Power, Subjectivity and Context in Workplace Bullying, Emotional Abuse and Harassment: Insights from Postpositivism." *Qualitative Research in Organizations and Management: An International Journal* 13, no. 1. Bradford, West Yorkshire: Emerald, 2018.

De Luca, Michael, Rachael Horovitz, Brad Pitt, Scott Rudin, Andrew Karsch, Sidney Kimmel, Mark Bakshi, et al. *Moneyball*. Culver City, CA: Sony Pictures Home Entertainment, 2012.

Denborough, David. *Retelling the Stories of Our Lives: Everyday Narrative Therapy to Draw Inspiration and Transform Experience*. New York: Norton, 2014.

Devine, Tom, Tarek F. Maassarani, and Government Accountability Project. *The Corporate Whistleblower's Survival Guide: A Handbook for Committing the Truth*. San Francisco: Berrett-Koehler, 2011.

Duffy, Maureen P., and Len Sperry. *Mobbing: Causes, Consequences, and Solutions.* Oxford: Oxford University Press, 2012.

———. *Overcoming Mobbing: A Recovery Guide for Workplace Aggression and Bullying.* Oxford: Oxford University Press, 2013.

Dzurec, Laura Cox. "Examining 'Sticky' Storytelling and Moral Claims as the Essence of Workplace Bullying." *Nursing Outlook* 68, no. 5 (2020): 647–56.

Edmondson, Amy. *The Fearless Organization: Creating Psychological Safety in the Workplace for Learning, Innovation, and Growth.* Hoboken, NJ: Wiley, 2019.

Edwards, Carolyn Pope, Lella Gandini, and George E. Forman. *The Hundred Languages of Children: The Reggio Emilia Experience in Transformation.* Santa Barbara, CA: Praeger, 2012.

Einarsen, Ståle. "The Nature and Causes of Bullying." *International Journal of Manpower,* 20 (1999): 16–27.

Einarsen, Ståle, Helge Hoel, Dieter Zapf, and Cary L Cooper, eds. *Bullying and Harassment in the Workplace: Theory, Research and Practice,* 3rd ed. Abingdon, Oxon: Routledge, 2020.

Ellis, Carolyn, Tony E. Adams, and Arthur P. Bochner. "Autoethnography: An Overview." *Historical Social Research/Historische Sozialforschung* 36, no. 4 (138) (2011): 273–90.

Epstein, David J. *Range: Why Generalists Triumph in a Specialized World.* New York: Riverhead, 2021.

Feng, Jie, Yucheng Zhang, Xinmei Liu, Long Zhang, and Xiao Han. "Just the Right Amount of Ethics Inspires Creativity: A Cross-Level Investigation of Ethical Leadership, Intrinsic Motivation, and Employee Creativity." *Journal of Business Ethics,* 153 (2018): 645–58.

Floridi, Luciano. "Faultless Responsibility: On the Nature and Allocation of Moral Responsibility for Distributed Moral Actions." *Philosophical Transactions: Mathematical, Physical and Engineering Sciences* 374, no. 2083 (2016): 1–13.

Fosslien, Liz, and Mollie West Duffy. *No Hard Feelings: The Secret Power of Embracing Emotions at Work.* New York: Portfolio, 2019.

Frankl, Viktor E. *Man's Search for Meaning: An Introduction to Logotherapy,* 4th ed. Cutchogue, NY: Buccaneer Books, 1992.

Garfinkel, Harold. (1956). "Conditions of Successful Degradation Ceremonies." *American Journal of Sociology* 61, no. 5 (1956): 420–24.

Goffman, Erving. *Stigma: Notes on the Management of Spoiled Identity.* New York: Simon & Schuster, 1963.

Gruenewald, Tara, Margaret Kemeny, Najib Aziz, and John Fahey. "Acute Threat to the Social Self: Shame, Social Self-Esteem, and Cortisol Activity." *Psychosomatic Medicine,* 66 (2004): 915–24.

Hallberg, Lillemor R. M., and Margaretha K. Strandmark. "Health Consequences of Workplace Bullying: Experiences from the Perspective of

Employees in the Public Service Sector." *International Journal of Qualitative Research* 1, no. 2 (2006): 109–19.

Hamilton, Patrick. *Gas Light: A Victorian Thriller in Three Acts.* London: Constable, 1939.

Hampton, D., K. Tharp-Barrie, and M. Kay Rayens. "Experience of Nursing Leaders with Workplace Bullying and How to Best Cope." *Journal of Nursing Management* 27, no. 3 (2019): 517–26.

Hansen, Åse Marie. *Workplace Bullying, Stress Response and Long Term Sickness Absence-Exploring Mechanisms: Results from Six Cohort Studies.* Copenhagen: Faculty of Health and Medical Sciences, University of Copenhagen, 2017.

Hare, Robert. *Without Conscience: The Disturbing World of the Psychopaths among Us.* New York: Pocket Books, 1993.

Hoel, Helge, Charlotte Rayner, and Cary Cooper. "Workplace Bullying." *International Review of Industrial Organizational Psychology,* 14 (1999): 195–229.

Hoever, Inga, J. Zhou, and Daan Knippenberg. "Different Strokes for Different Teams: The Contingent Effects of Positive and Negative Feedback on the Creativity of Informationally Homogeneous and Diverse Teams." *Academy of Management Journal* 61, no. 6 (2017): 2159–81.

Hontvedt, Magnus, Kenneth Silseth, and Line Wittek. "Professional Collaboration in Teacher Support Teams—A Study of Teacher and Nurse Educators' Creative Problem-Solving in a Shared Space for Professional Development." *Scandinavian Journal of Educational Research* 65, no. 2 (2021): 240–57.

Hu, Jia, Berrin Erdogan, Kaifeng Jiang, Talya N. Bauer, and Songbo Liu. "Leader Humility and Team Creativity: The Role of Team Information Sharing, Psychological Safety, and Power Distance." *Journal of Applied Psychology* 103, no. 3 (2018): 313–23.

Janoff-Bulman, Ronnie. *Shattered Assumptions: Towards a New Psychology of Trauma.* New York: Simon & Schuster, 2010.

Janssens, Heidi, Lutgart Braeckman, Bart De Clercq, Annalisa Casini, Dirk De Bacquer, France Kittel, and Els Clays. "The Indirect Association of Job Strain with Long-Term Sickness Absence through Bullying: A Mediation Analysis Using Structural Equation Modeling." *BMC Public Health* 16, no. 1 (2016): 851–51.

Jennings, Ken. "The Origin of the Phrase 'Beyond the Pale.'" October 10, 2016, https://www.cntraveler.com/story/what-beyond-the-pale-actually.

Jones, Eric, and Janice Kelly. "'Why Am I Out of the Loop?' Attributions Influence Responses to Information Exclusion." *Personality and Social Psychology Bulletin* 36, no. 9 (2010): 1186–1201.

Joseph, Stephen. *What Doesn't Kill Us: The New Psychology of Posttraumatic Growth.* New York: Basic Books, 2011.

Kenny, Kate. *Whistleblowing: Toward a New Theory.* Cambridge, MA: Harvard University Press, 2019.

Kessler, David. *Finding Meaning: The Sixth Stage of Grief.* New York: Scribner, 2020.

Kiecolt-Glaser, Janice K. "Marriage, Divorce, and the Immune System." *American Psychologist* 73, no. 9 (2018): 1098–1108.

Kim, Tae-Yeol, Jie Wang, and Junsong Chen. "Mutual Trust between Leader and Subordinate and Employee Outcomes." *Journal of Business Ethics* 149, no. 4 (2018): 945–58.

Kohn, Alfie. "Digging Themselves in Deeper: More Misleading Claims about the Value of Homework." *Phi Delta Kappan* 88, no. 7 (2007): 514–17.

Konnikova, Maria. "Messy: The Power of Disorder to Transform Our Lives by Tim Harford." *New York Times Book Review* 121, no. 42 (2016): 21–21.

Kübler-Ross, Elisabeth. *On Death and Dying.* New York: Collier Books, 1993.

Kumai, Candice. *Kintsugi Wellness: The Japanese Art of Nourishing Mind, Body, and Soul.* New York: HarperCollins, 2018.

Kushner, Harold S. *When Bad Things Happen to Good People.* New York: Schocken, 1981.

Lateef, Fatimah. "Maximizing Learning and Creativity: Understanding Psychological Safety in Simulation-Based Learning." *Journal of Emergencies, Trauma, and Shock* 13, no. 1 (2020): 5–14.

Leach, Liana S., Carmel Poyser, and Peter Butterworth. "Workplace Bullying and the Association with Suicidal Ideation/Thoughts and Behaviour: A Systematic Review." *Occupational and Environmental Medicine* 74, no. 1 (2017): 72–79.

Lever, Isabel, Daniel Dyball, Neil Greenberg, and Sharon A. M. Stevelink. "Health Consequences of Bullying in the Healthcare Workplace: A Systematic Review." *Journal of Advanced Nursing* 75, no. 12 (2019): 3195–3209.

Levin, Ira. *The Stepford Wives.* New York: Random House, 1972.

Lewis, Duncan. "Bullying at Work: The Impact of Shame among University and College Lecturers." *British Journal of Guidance & Counselling* 32, no. 3 (2004): 281–99.

Leymann, Heinz. "Mobbing and Psychological Terror at Workplaces." *Violence and Victims* 5, no. 2 (1990): 119–26.

Locke, Leslie Ann, and Sonya D. Hayes. "Navigating the Gendered Labyrinths and Managing the Mean Girls and Queen Bees within the Academy: A Dialogue between Two Women Assistant Professors." *Sojo Journal: Educational Foundations and Social Justice Education* 6, nos. 1–2 (2020): 41–55.

Lo Presti, Alessandro, Paolo Pappone, and Alfonso Landolfi. "The Associations between Workplace Bullying and Physical or Psychological Negative Symptoms: Anxiety and Depression as Mediators." *Europe's Journal of Psychology* 15, no. 4 (2019): 808–22.

Lorenz, Konrad. *Aggression: Background and Nature.* Stockholm: Norstedt & Söner, 1966.

Magee, Christopher, Ross Gordon, Laura Robinson, Peter Caputi, and Lindsay Oades. "Workplace Bullying and Absenteeism: The Mediating Roles of Poor Health and Work Engagement." *Human Resource Management Journal* 27, no. 3 (2017): 319–34.

Mainert, Jakob, Christoph Niepel, Kevin R. Murphy, and Samuel Greiff. "The Incremental Contribution of Complex Problem-Solving Skills to the Prediction of Job Level, Job Complexity, and Salary." *Journal of Business and Psychology* 34, no. 6 (2019): 825–45.

Malik, Naima Akhtar, and Kaj Björkqvist. "Workplace Bullying and Occupational Stress among University Teachers: Mediating and Moderating Factors." *Europe's Journal of Psychology*, 2 (2019): 240–59.

Mao, Y., C. Jiang, Y. Liu, and I. D. Zhang. "Why Am I Ostracized and How Would I React? A Review of Workplace Ostracism Research." *Asia Pacific Journal of Management* 35, no. 3 (2018): 745–67.

Martinez, Mario E. *The Mindbody Code: How to Change the Beliefs That Limit Your Health, Longevity, and Success.* Boulder, CO: Sounds True, 2016.

———. *The Mindbody Self: How Longevity Is Culturally Learned and the Causes of Health Are Inherited.* Carlsbad, CA: Hay House, 2017.

McClure, John, and James Brown. "Belonging at Work." *Human Resource Development International* 11, no. 1 (2008): 3–17.

Mesmer-Magnus, Jessica R., and Chockalingam Viswesvaran. "Whistleblowing in Organizations: An Examination of Correlates of Whistleblowing Intentions, Actions, and Retaliation." *Journal of Business Ethics* 62, no. 3 (2005): 277–97.

Meyers, Maria Christina, Byron G. Adams, Lusanda Sekaja, Carmen Buzea, Ana-Maria Cazan, Mihaela Gotea, Delia Stefenel, and Marianne van Woerkom. "Perceived Organizational Support for the Use of Employees' Strengths and Employee Well-Being: A Cross-Country Comparison." *Journal of Happiness Studies: An Interdisciplinary Forum on Subjective Well-Being* 20, no. 6 (2019): 1825–41.

Michailova, Snejina, and Kenneth Husted. "Knowledge-Sharing Hostility in Russian Firms." *California Management Review* 45, no. 3 (2003): 59–77.

Moffat, Wendy. "Creativity and Collaboration in the Small College Department." *Pedagogy* 10, no. 2 (2010): 283–94.

Morgan, Alice. *What Is Narrative Therapy? An Easy-to-Read Introduction.* Adelaide, South Australia: Dulwich Centre, 2000.

Morningstar, Dana. *Out of the Fog: Moving from Confusion to Clarity after Narcissistic Abuse.* Mason, MI: Morningstar Media, 2018.

Murray, Donald. "The Maker's Eye." In B. Ballenger, ed., *The Curious Writer.* New York: Pearson, 2004, 421–25.

Nabe-Nielsen, Kirsten, Matias Brødsgaard Grynderup, Theis Lange, Johan Hviid Andersen, Jens Peter Bonde, Paul Maurice Conway, Anne Helene

Garde, et al. "The Role of Poor Sleep in the Relation between Workplace Bullying/Unwanted Sexual Attention and Long-Term Sickness Absence." *International Archives of Occupational and Environmental Health* 89, no. 6 (2016): 967–79.

Namie, Gary. *U.S. Workplace Bullying Survey*, Workplace Bullying Institute, Zogby Analytics (pollster), 2021.

Namie, G., and R. Namie. *The Bully-Free Workplace: Stop Jerks, Weasels, and Snakes from Killing Your Organization*. Hoboken, NJ: Wiley, 2011.

Nascimento, Susana, and Pólvora Alexandre. "Maker Cultures and the Prospects for Technological Action." *Science and Engineering Ethics* 24, no. 3 (2018): 927–46.

National Workplace Bullying Coalition. https://www.workplacebullying-coalition.org. Accessed August 1, 2022.

Near, Janet P., and Marcia P. Miceli. "Organizational Dissidence: The Case of Whistle-Blowing." *Journal of Business Ethics* 4, no. 1 (1985): 1–16.

Ng, Catalina Sau Man. "Effects of Workplace Bullying on Chinese Children's Health, Behaviours and School Adjustment Via Parenting: Study Protocol for a Longitudinal Study." *BMC Public Health* 19, no. 1 (2019): 1–12.

Nielsen, Morten Birkeland, Marianne Skogbrott Birkeland, Marianne Bang Hansen, Stein Knardahl, and Trond Heir. "Victimization from Workplace Bullying after a Traumatic Event: Time-Lagged Relationships with Symptoms of Posttraumatic Stress." *International Archives of Occupational and Environmental Health* 90, no. 5 (2017): 411–21.

Nielsen, Morten Birkeland, Geir Høstmark Nielsen, Guy Notelaers, and Ståle Einarsen. "Workplace Bullying and Suicidal Ideation: A 3-Wave Longitudinal Norwegian Study." *American Journal of Public Health* 105, no. 11 (2015): 23–28.

Nietzsche, Friedrich Wilhelm. *Twilight of the Idols*. Dover Thrift Editions. Mineola, NY: Dover, 2019.

Okri, Ben. *A Way of Being Free*. London: Head of Zeus, 2014.

Orkodashvili, Mariam. "Corruption, Collusion, and Nepotism in Higher Education and the Labor Market in Georgia." *European Education* 43, no. 2 (2011): 32–53.

Padgett, Margaret Y., Robert J. Padgett, and Kathryn A. Morris. "Perceptions of Nepotism Beneficiaries: The Hidden Price of Using a Family Connection to Obtain a Job." *Journal of Business and Psychology* 30, no. 2 (2015): 283–98.

Patterson, Kerry. *Crucial Conversation: Tools for Talking When Stakes Are High*. New York: McGraw-Hill, 2002.

Paulhus, Delroy L., and Kevin M. Williams. "The Dark Triad of Personality: Narcissism, Machiavellianism, and Psychopathy." *Journal of Research in Personality* 36, no. 6 (2002): 556–63.

Pelias, Ronald. *A Poetics of Personal Relations*. Walnut Creek, CA: Left Coast Press, 2011.

Pennebaker, James. "The Effects of Traumatic Disclosure on Physical and Mental Health: The Values of Writing and Talking about Upsetting Events." *International Journal of Emergency Mental Health* 1, no. 1 (1999): 9–18.

Pennebaker, James, and John Evans. *Expressive Writing: Words That Heal*. Enumclaw, WA: Idyll Arbor, 2014.

Perkins, David N. *The Mind's Best Work*. Cambridge, MA: Harvard University Press, 1981.

Philips, Deborah. "Gaslighting: Domestic Noir, the Narratives of Coercive Control." *Women: A Cultural Review* 32, no. 2 (2021): 140–60.

Pouwelse, Mieneke, Roelie Mulder, Eva Gemzøe Mikkelsen, P. D'Cruz, E. Noronha, E. Baillien, B. Catley, K. Harlos, A. Hogh, and E. Gemzøe Mikkelsen. "Pathways of Job-Related Negative Behavior: Handbooks of Workplace Bullying, Emotional Abuse and Harassment," 2, 1–37. Essay. In *The Role of Bystanders in Workplace Bullying: An Overview of Theories and Empirical Research*. New York: Springer, 2019, 6–27. Rees, McKenzie R., Ann E. Tenbrunsel, and Max H. Bazerman. "Bounded Ethicality and Ethical Fading in Negotiations: Understanding Unintended Unethical Behavior." *Academy of Management Perspectives* 33, no. 1 (2019): 26–42.

Rosander, Michael, Denise Salin, and Stefan Blomberg. "The Last Resort: Workplace Bullying and the Consequences of Changing Jobs." *Scandinavian Journal of Psychology* 63, no. 2 (2022): 124–35.

Rowling, J. K. *Harry Potter and the Sorcerer's Stone*. New York: Scholastic, 1998.

Rozovsky, Julie. "The Five Keys to a Successful Google Team." In *re:Work*, November 17, 2015. https://rework.withgoogle.com/blog/five-keys-to-a-successful-google-team.

Seligman, Martin E. P., and Mihaly Csikszentmihalyi. "Positive Psychology: An Introduction." *American Psychologist* 55, no. 1 (2000): 5–14.

Sherman, Arie, and Tal Shavit. "The Thrill of Creative Effort at Work: An Empirical Study on Work, Creative Effort and Well-Being." *Journal of Happiness Studies: An Interdisciplinary Forum on Subjective Well-Being* 19, no. 7 (2018): 2049–69.

Solas, John. "Conscientious Objections to Corporate Wrongdoing." *Business and Society Review* 124, no. 1 (2019): 43–62. https://doi.org/10.1111/basr.12162.

Star Wars. Lucasfilm Ltd, 2000.

Starks, Helene, and Susan Brown Trinidad. "Choose Your Method: A Comparison of Phenomenology, Discourse Analysis, and Grounded Theory." *Qualitative Health Research* 17, no. 10 (2007): 1372–80.

Suskind, Dorothy. *Bully-Wise: From Surviving to Thriving*, July 28, 2022. https://www.psychologytoday.com/us/blog/bully-wise.

———. "Writing: An Act of Revolution." *English Journal* 111, no. 4 (2022): 17–19.

Tatar, Zeynep Baran, and Yüksel Şahika. "Mobbing at Workplace: Psychological Trauma and Documentation of Psychiatric Symptoms." *Archives of Neuropsychiatry* 56, no. 1 (2019): 57–62.

Tedeschi, Richard G. *Posttraumatic Growth: Theory, Research and Applications.* New York: Routledge, 2018.

Tedeschi, Richard G., and Lawrence G. Calhoun. "Posttraumatic Growth: Conceptual Foundations and Empirical Evidence." *Psychological Inquiry* 15, no. 1 (2004): 1–18.

———. "The Posttraumatic Growth Inventory: Measuring the Positive Legacy of Trauma." *Journal of Traumatic Stress* 9, no. 3 (1996): 455–71.

Tong, Myriam, Rene Schwendimann, and Franziska Zúñiga. "Mobbing among Care Workers in Nursing Homes: A Cross-Sectional Secondary Analysis of the Swiss Nursing Homes Human Resources Project." *International Journal of Nursing Studies*, 66 (2017): 72–81.

Verkuil, B., S. Atasayi, and M. L. Molendijk. "Workplace Bullying and Mental Health: A Meta-Analysis on Cross-Sectional and Longitudinal Data," *PLoS One* 10, no. 8 (2015), https://doi.org/1156 10.1371/journal.pone.0135225.

Waltz, Lee Ann, Laura Muñoz, Holly Weber Johnson, and Tracy Rodriguez. "Exploring Job Satisfaction and Workplace Engagement in Millennial Nurses." *Journal of Nursing Management* 28, no. 3 (2020): 673–81.

Westhues, Ken. *The Envy of Excellence: Administrative Mobbing of High-Achieving Professors.* Lewiston, NY: Tribunal for Academic Justice/Edwin Mellen Press, 2005.

White, Michael. *Narrative Practice: Continuing the Conversation.* New York: Norton, 2011.

Williams, Kipling D., and Lisa Zadro. "Interpersonal Rejection." *In Ostracism: On Being Ignored, Excluded, and Rejected.* Oxford, UK: Oxford University Press, 2006.

Workplace Bullying. *National Workplace Bullying Coalition.* https://www.workplacebullyingcoalition.org. August 1, 2022.

Workplace Bullying Institute. https://workplacebullying.org. Accessed August 1, 2022.

Index

About the Author

Dorothy Suskind is a writer, researcher, and assistant professor in the Education and Counseling Department at Longwood University in Farmville, Virginia. At Longwood, she directs the Southside Virginia Writing Project, part of the National Writing Project, and teaches a variety of classes in literacy and a capstone course titled Women as Disruptive Change Agents in Their Community. Before coming to Longwood, she served as a teacher, reading specialist, middle school principal, action research coach, and assistant professor at the University of Mary Washington. Dorothy earned a BA and MEd from Virginia Commonwealth University and a PhD from the University of Virginia. She researches and writes on a variety of topics, including workplace bullying, bullying in childhood and adolescents, sexual assault, creativity, healthy work cultures, and women in the workplace. Dorothy resides in Richmond, Virginia, with her husband, Greg, and two beloved boys, Mac and Charlie.